The Stars for Sam

by W. Maxwell Reed

THE EARTH FOR SAM

THE SEA FOR SAM
(with Wilfrid S. Bronson)

AND THAT'S WHY

THE SKY IS BLUE

AMERICA'S TREASURE

THE

Revised Edition

Edited by PAUL F. BRANDWEIN

Illustrated with photographs

Harcourt, Brace and Company NEW YORK

W. MAXWELL REED

Stars FOR SAM

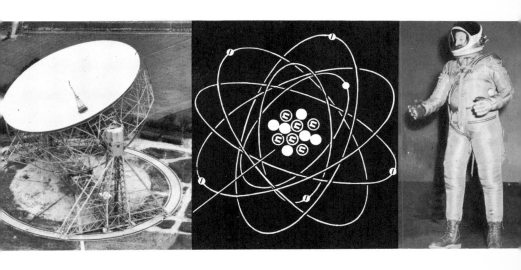

Contents

Editor's Note

Sam first heard the story of the stars from his uncle, W. Maxwell Reed. In revising the original story, we have had the invaluable help of Professor Fletcher G. Watson of Harvard University, and Dr. T. D. Nicholson, Astronomer, Hayden Planetarium, The American Museum of Natural History, New York City. Our purpose has been a clear one: to retain the qualities that made *The Stars for Sam* so appealing to so many young people over the years.

PAUL F. BRANDWEIN

The Stars for Sam

Foreword

Daedalus and his son Icarus — if they were alive today — would volunteer to be the first men in any experimental spaceship. Myth or not, Daedalus and his son, you remember, were the first to try flight — with wings fastened to their shoulders by wax. But Icarus, alas, did not heed his father's plea not to fly too high, not to dare the sun's heat because it would melt the wax. He did fly high toward the sun, and legend tells us the sun's heat melted the wax that secured his wings — and he plunged to his death.

But not the children of today. They will fly. They already fly on planes. The moon has been hit by a man-made missile. The first spaceman has already been born and, in the United States, seven astronauts have already been chosen. Soon one of them, or an astronaut from another land, may indeed become the first spaceman.

What will he need for his equipment? Not only the gift of high intelligence and a magnificent body — but also knowledge of the earth's neighbors in space.

His contemporaries will want to plot his course, follow him in their imaginations, and so they will turn their eyes to the stars.

1

The Sun — Your Star

Go out any bright sunny day and look for a star. Most people would say that you cannot find a star during the day, but the daylight star is there for all to see; it is the sun.

The sun must have been the first heavenly body to attract attention at the very dawn of intelligence in the animal kingdom. It was the mysterious giver of light and heat, and mysterious it still is. It is beyond our power to imagine what the heat of the sun and its dazzling brilliancy would be if we were near it. We know that the temperature of the surface of the sun is about 10,000° Fahrenheit, but the heat at the center of the sun is estimated to be about 35,000,000° Fahrenheit. Such figures mean very little to any of us unless we know that steel melts at about 4,500° Fahrenheit. All we can say is that the sun is so hot that it would be dangerous to get much nearer to it than we are at present.

That the sun is round was probably one of the first astronomical discoveries ever made. You can make that discovery yourself by looking at the sun at sunset on any clear day.

In early ages, men believed that the sun rose in the east

and set in the west, and we still speak of it as doing just that. We know now, however, that it does nothing of the sort. The motion we "see" belongs to the earth, which is spinning on its own axis. And as it spins, it turns toward and then away from the sun. A person at a spot on the earth turning at that moment toward the sun sees it "rise." As the day proceeds, the earth continues its spinning, and at nightfall the observer, now spinning with the earth away from the sun, sees it set.

Copernicus of Poland was the first modern astronomer to put forth the idea that the earth revolves around the sun. Only much later were we to discover that the sun is really big enough to contain over a million earths.

The sun was considered to be absolutely perfect by our ancestors who lived in Europe during the Dark Ages, which followed the fall of Rome. It is easy to see why they regarded it as a brilliant sphere without a flaw. Whether we look at the setting sun through the dust-laden air or, by means of smoked glass, at the dazzling light of the noonday sun, we almost always see a flawless disc. Apparently it has clean-cut edges and is as smooth as a lens. Imagine the surprise when Galileo, who lived in the late sixteenth and early seventeenth centuries — the first person to look at the sun through a telescope — found several black spots on its surface (Figure 1-1).

This discovery made Galileo very unpopular. He had destroyed an ideal. It was as bad as criticizing a hero. Nowadays, however, we want to find out all we can about the sun, and the more we discover, the more wonderful that source of light appears to be.

Through a large telescope, the surface of the sun looks like a mass of clouds, each of which is at least one hundred,

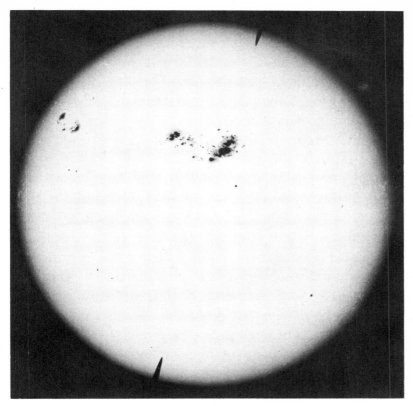

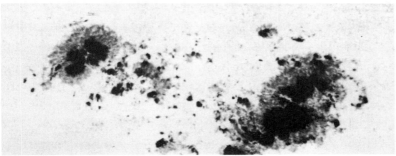

Figure 1-1. Above is the disc of the sun with a clear set of sunspots. Below are the sunspots closer up. The spots are masses of swirling hot gas. Scientists are studying sunspots to discover how they affect the earth's atmosphere and its life.

(Mount Wilson and Palomar Observatories)

and sometimes several hundred, miles across. These are not clouds of rain or snow — condensed vapors like the clouds in our atmosphere — but masses of shining hot vapor — gases of hydrogen and helium, plus some iron, lead, tin, and other substances in gaseous form. These gases are of different temperatures, some expanding and some rising, others contracting and falling.

From cool and quiet observatories on the earth we look across a space of over ninety million miles and into a great hot ball — hotter than anything we can describe. Flare-ups of heated material, greater than any volcanic outburst or even an atomic bomb, are taking place continually. There is no clear-cut surface to this sea of fire. Gases of different degrees of heat, even of different substances, are thought to be moving outward from the sun's interior. At the outer part the heated atmosphere must become cooler, but it is still hotter than anything we know. The surface of the sun is then, to some extent, an optical illusion. It is not sharply defined — it is a mass of gases, with eruptions every now and then.

Those innocent black spots that Galileo saw for the first time are masses of gas that flow out over the part of the sun that looks to us like a surface. As they rush up from the interior and overflow in all directions, they never rise more than five hundred miles from the imaginary surface of the sun called the photosphere (sphere of light).

Through our telescopes we look down upon these columns of gas from the top. They rise so rapidly that they have cooled to some extent. In contrast to the layers of incandescent vapor around them, they look actually black.

The flowing of the sunspot gas over the surface of the photosphere causes a very curious thing to take place.

There is nothing on the earth that is exactly like this queer thing, and therefore it is a little difficult to understand. The intensely hot substances of which the sun is made give off such bright light that atoms and atomic particles, free to move, are driven away because light, like wind, has a force that can blow away extremely tiny particles. Even an ordinary candle flame has such a repelling power, but it is so feeble that you don't realize it. If, however, you were a tiny atom and if you were near the terrifically hot and brilliant sun, then you would feel the repelling force of light.

Stretching far out beyond the sun, sometimes several million miles, is a halo called the "corona" (Figure 1-2). It looks something like a glorified display of "northern lights." Just what it is we do not know. It is a gas, and it probably is an excessively rarefied one — more nearly resembling our idea of a vacuum than a gas. Perhaps it is in part the illuminated portion of a great cloud of celestial particles. The arrangement of these particles may have been distorted by the magnetic attraction of the sun into long filaments, which, when illuminated, give the appearance we see in the photograph (Figure 1-2).

The solar eruptions that cause sunspots last much longer than, say, a tornado on the earth. They usually are visible for many days and sometimes for months. It was by watching these long-enduring solar storms that we first discovered that the sun was turning on its axis like the earth. The sun, about 864,000 miles in diameter, turns much more slowly than the earth, making one rotation in about twenty-five days. It twists on its axis in the same direction in which the earth goes around the sun. If we could look down upon the sun, moon, and earth, we would see the sun twisting on its axis in the opposite way from the hands of a clock. The earth would be seen running around the sun, also counterclockwise, and at the same time spinning on its axis in the same direction. We would see that the moon circles around the earth counterclockwise as well. And we could not fail to note that all the planets — Mercury, Venus, Mars, Jupiter, Saturn, Uranus, Neptune, and Pluto — travel around the sun, all counterclockwise (Figure 1-3).

Once in a while the moon, in its counterclockwise journey around the earth, comes directly between us and the sun (Figure 1-2). For a few seconds the sun is completely hidden — eclipsed. Then we can see what is happening on the edge of the sun. Ordinarily the sun is so dazzlingly bright that we cannot see its atmosphere. Also when the sun

Figure 1-2. The sun's corona. The brilliant crown was photographed when the sun's disc was eclipsed by the moon; otherwise the corona couldn't be seen. Notice the hairlike edges of the corona. (*Official United States Navy Photograph*)

is setting in the west, the same dust that enables us to see it apparently as a round red ball prevents us from seeing its atmosphere. Sometimes the sun is only partly eclipsed; then it appears as in Figure 1-4.

During an eclipse, the blinding light of the sun is temporarily hidden behind the moon. Then we see the brilliant solar atmosphere. Huge eruptions, called prominences, are

Figure 1-3.   The solar family. The arrows indicate the direction in which the nine planets move. Notice the small bodies (asteroids) between Mars and Jupiter. What happens when the moon gets in between the earth and the sun? (*Drawing by Mildred Waltrip from* You and Science *by Brandwein, Beck, Hollingworth, and Burgess, copyright, 1950, 1952, 1955 by Harcourt, Brace and Company, Inc.*)

Figure 1-4.   Sometimes the sun is not completely eclipsed by the moon as shown in the photograph in Figure 1-2. Here is a partial eclipse of the sun as seen at 6 A.M., September 1, 1951, over Washington, D.C.

(United Press International Photo)

seen on the sun's surface (Figure 1-5). These prominences are enormously high — one hundred thousand miles, or more. Of course, they are appearing and disappearing and changing their fantastic shapes but too slowly for the eye to see. They always contain incandescent hydrogen, a gas that shines with red light at the high temperature of the sun.

Astronomers are really beginning now to get information on the nature of the sun's light and heat — its tremendous energy. As you study more science, you will learn that the sun is not only the source of our light and heat but also is the source of all the energy we use — even our food. To be too far away from the sun means death by freezing; to be too near means death by burning. The planet Mercury is too near the sun; Pluto is too far. Our own planet, the earth, seems to be just about the right distance away from the sun for life to flourish.

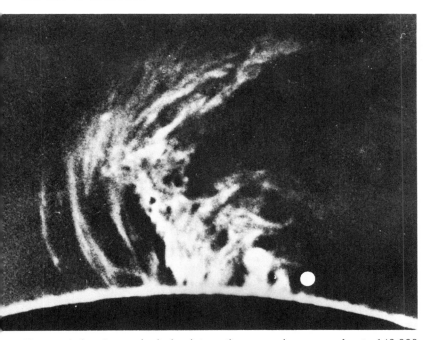

Figure 1-5. A particularly interesting prominence — about 140,000 miles high. Astronomers are studying these huge eruptions of gas carefully to find out the make-up of the sun.

(Mount Wilson and Palomar Observatories)

2

Our Platform in Space—and Its Moon

Every day adds new names to the hardware in the sky — Sputnik, Explorer, Pioneer, Atlas, Titan, and so forth; moon-shoot follows moon-shoot. The Russian rocket, Lunik II, hit the moon; Lunik III circled it. But in one sense man is merely copying nature. We are on a relatively permanent platform in space. And we might say it "blasted off" the sun some billions of years ago; some scientists say about six billions of years ago. Others think it's safer not to say, because we really don't know.

Of course, you may not have thought of the earth as a platform in space — or a space station. But think a moment. It is in space; it is a kind of "satellite" of the sun with an orbit around it. And you are on it, hurtling around the sun at an incredible speed of eighteen miles per second.

Let us scan the sky for the body nearest our earth. Aside from a man-made moon or so, it is our natural moon. To find out about the origin of the moon, we need first to find out about the origin of the earth, for one idea is that our moon came from the earth. One theory of the origin of the earth, no longer very popular, goes something like this in its major details.

There are over 10,000 million stars (in a group of stars called the Milky Way) of which our sun — our star, if you will — is a part. Those millions and thousands of millions of stars that make up the Milky Way are not by any means stationary. They are moving with a speed of many miles per second. We should expect that two stars might occasionally come so close as to cause great tidal waves on each other's surface. In short, with about 10,000 million stars in the group, they might occasionally come almost near enough to sideswipe each other.

This theory goes on to suggest that the sun and a wandering star dashed past each other and gigantic waves were raised on each. The waves were so great that they splashed right out into space. A vast amount of the stuff of which the sun is made was thrown away from the surface with such force that it could not return.

According to this theory, a portion of the ejected matter began to revolve around the sun in oval orbits. It was spread out like a flat disc, and from a great distance it may have looked something like Saturn's rings. The modern rings of Saturn are, however, smoother than were the great parent rings from which the planets came. At first, they probably looked something like a stream of clouds.

However fiery hot this matter had originally been when it left the sun, most of it became so cold as to freeze in a comparatively short time. Quantities of gases of various kinds were held prisoner inside these pieces of the badly damaged sun, but, of course, it is thought that a great deal of free gas was blown away by the temporarily intense brilliance of the sunlight. We say "temporarily," because the sun was made unusually bright by the disturbing effect of that passing star. Before long, however, the sun cooled a bit and recovered from the encounter. Thus its unusual brilliance was but a temporary glow. If the sun had been accompanied by a previous set of planets, they would have been scorched beyond recognition.

We do not know what companions, if any, the sun had before this primeval and, for us, historic encounter; but one theory would have us believe that from the welter of this catastrophe Venus, Earth, Mars, and the other planets emerged. Life ultimately arose on at least one of these planets and perhaps — a very great perhaps — on three of them.

For millions and thousands of millions of years this curious procession of large and small bodies of rock and metal continued their endless journey around the sun. Gradually the sun lost its unnatural and perhaps pulsating brilliancy and became the source of the almost steady and moderate light we know so well.

Do not think that these millions of annual trips around the sun by the pieces of rock and metal were uneventful. Collisions were the order of the day. Sometimes they came together to form swarms of individual rocks. Then on other occasions they would hit each other with such force as to become welded together. In this way some of the big aggregations grew bigger, for they attracted the little fellows to them. At the same time, perhaps, many of the little fellows were growing bigger also; but they couldn't catch up with the few big ones that had a good and early start.

Perhaps the big masses of metal and rock were liquid at first and in a few million years cooled enough to form a hard crust. No matter how hard that crust was, it would not have been a good place to live. First, there would have been no atmosphere of any kind and certainly no free oxygen. There would have been cracks on the surface of such a mass, and some of the hot interior would have flowed through these cracks and over the surface. Many of these eruptions we would have called volcanoes, and as with volcanoes today, many gases escaped from the boiling lava. Today these gases give us nitrogen, water vapor, and carbon dioxide; but years ago the masses of rock and metal were probably too small to hold the gases. These little molecules of gas, as they became heated by sunlight, developed a speed so great that they could not stay on the primeval ball. They bounced away almost as fast as they came from the boiling lava. Once clear of the growing ball's immediate attraction, the intense sunlight probably drove them off to the endless stretches of interstellar space.

The second reason why life on such an early mass of meteoric stuff would not have been happy was the danger of being struck by other masses of rock and metal. For millions of years the surface of these barren globes of rock and iron must have resembled a no-man's-land. The bigger the ball grew, the more it gathered to itself the neighboring rocks. Some were large, and millions were small; but the impacts dented the surface into craters and splashed molten rock in all directions.

Gradually, by means of these impacts, the large masses grew even larger and ultimately became the planets, from Mercury to Pluto. When they became large, their power to attract an atmosphere increased. Then the heated and vibrating atoms of gas from the boiling lava could no longer bounce away. They remained on the planet's surface and formed an atmosphere. Thus for most of the planets a new epoch in their history commenced, for with the exception of Mercury they continued ever after to go through the universe surrounded by a halo of gas, an atmosphere.

Perhaps some of the globes in the very beginning were so large that they had an atmosphere. Such may have been the history of Jupiter, Saturn, Uranus, and Neptune. It is even possible that the earth had a small atmosphere from the very first.

Another more recent theory, conceived by the astronomer Fred Whipple, would describe the origin of the earth somewhat like this. The sun and its planets, our solar system, were first part of a huge whirling cloud of gas. For some reason, not yet fully determined, this cloud of gas collapsed and, as it did so, formed a central "nucleus," which eventually became our sun, and scattered nuclei of material that became first planets or "protoplanets" as they have been called. These small planets, or first planets, being of greater mass, pulled in other bits of swirling material. Thus they became ever larger. Slowly they cooled and became the planets and moons as we know them now.

Some scientists consider this theory more satisfying because it explains more of the facts as we know them now. As additional facts are gathered, new theories are formed to explain them. You will learn that the facts are stubborn and it is the theories that are changed to fit them.

These are two explanations of the origin of the earth and its moon. There will, no doubt, be others during your lifetime.

It may be however, that our moon, due to its original speed and location, did not fall upon the earth but revolved around it instead. Thus it became the earth's partner and grew as the earth grew. New data resulting from explorations by space satellites will add to our knowledge; we will then know more about the moon and its origin.

Some think that the moon was once a part of the earth.

They assume that the earth emerged from the great side-swiping as a ball of liquid rock, iron, and the other substances it now contains. It was not so large as it is now; yet it was large enough to be unwieldy, and when it came near the sun in its annual journey, it was warped into a pear-shaped body by the tremendous forces, called tidal forces, of the sun and by the vibrations set up by the rapid spinning on its axis. In time it became something like a dumbbell with one lobe smaller than the other. Finally it broke, and now we call the smaller lobe the moon and the larger lobe the earth.

Harold Jeffreys of Cambridge University, England, thought that the sun and the passing star actually collided and that the moon never was a part of the earth but was merely one of the many primeval balls and ultimately became the earth's partner. He also thought that the catastrophe to which we owe our existence happened less than 10,000 million years ago.

However, since the moon is almost as big as Mercury, some believe it is a true planet, formed in the same way as the earth and later, as we have said, captured by the earth. Whatever its origin, the moon never became large enough to hold an atmosphere, and so, like Mercury, it is to this day thought to be a barren waste of rock exposed directly to the almost perfect vacuum of space.

The earth's atmosphere protects life by burning with its friction the millions of small bodies (meteors or "shooting stars") that reach it. When these meteors reach the earth, they are called meteorites. On the other hand, by causing rain and snow, the atmosphere wears away the mountains until only grassy plains and forests are left. In this way, those giant craters made by meteorites millions of years ago, if they ever existed on earth, have all been worn away and covered with soil and forests. Not a single ancient crater remains as a monument to the first epoch of the earth's history. The moon, however, has kept a record of its history. When the surface of the moon is dented, it stays dented. There is no atmosphere to carry globules of water into the sky. Therefore, no rain ever falls upon the crags and rocky deserts (Figure 2-1). No winds throw sand at the rocks. No vegeta-

Figure 2-1. If you were on the moon, this is what you might see — craggy mountains, deserts, and craters. And in the distance, 240,000 miles away — the earth.

(Hayden Planetarium, American Museum of Natural History)

tion eats into rocks. Yet the surface of the rocks on the moon may crumble, we think, due to the intense heat of sunshine during the long lunar day of two weeks and the equally intense cold of space during the long night. During the day the moon is seared by a temperature that runs to 250° Fahrenheit; at night it is chilled to minus 215°. This variation in heat may cause expansion and contraction so that large slabs from the surface of cliffs may have loosened and crashed to the base of the mountains.

Other than these "mountain slides" the absence of an atmosphere on the moon — and hence of weather — must mean that the jagged mountains have not been softened by erosion. For this reason alone, the moon's jagged mountains appear to be higher than any on earth. And the craters are huge. The crater Newton is so deep that Mount Everest, the earth's highest peak, would barely show at its top. Newton is so deep that its floor must be eternally frozen since no ray of light could ever reach it. However, there have been reports of "mists" in the bottom of certain craters. Are these "mists" dust? Are they indications of an atmosphere? Further study will yield more evidence.

The large lunar seas, as they are known, are not "seas" in our sense at all, but are probably seas of hardened lava. In size, they may be compared to our southwestern deserts.

Meteors, large and small, must be pelting the moon incessantly. No blanket of air destroys these shooting stars, as does the earth's atmosphere. No stream of sparks announces the approach of a meteor. Almost invisible and in perfect silence, they crash upon the lunar mountains. They must cause havoc, and after millions of years they probably have destroyed many a cliff.

Yet after all, this damage is slight when compared with the leveling action of rain and snow, rivers and glaciers. So the moon, which has none of these, has been little altered by the lapse of several thousand million years. If we examined it, we would find it dented by thousands of craters. Some are very small, and others are a few hundred miles in diameter. Some look like volcanoes, and perhaps they are volcanoes that once upon a time were active. Others are so large and the rims so low that they give the appearance of

great circular plains several hundred miles in diameter
(Figure 2-2).

We do not know that all the moon's craters were formed
by meteor bombardment. Some day the true cause of the
craters on the moon may be known.

That the moon is round is quite obvious. That it shines
by reflected light is perhaps not so self-evident. Yet if you

Figure 2-2.   The face of the moon. As the moon is studied more carefully, more of its features will become evident. The Russian rocket, Lunik
II, is said to have landed at the edge of the Sea of Tranquility. Next
time you see pictures of the moon, try to identify one or two different
places on it. A small telescope would, of course, give you some valuable
hours of discovery and fun.   *(Lick Observatory)*

look carefully at the moon, you will strongly suspect that it shines only by reflected sunlight, for you will notice that the bright side always is nearest to the sun.

We sometimes see the entire "sunny" side of the moon, which we call the full moon. About one week earlier than full moon we can see only one-half the sunny side. We call this appearance the "first quarter" (Figure 2-3). At the most we see only 59 per cent of the moon's surface; the other side is permanently away from our view. One of the objectives in sending a satellite around the moon is to gain some idea of the other side. Through a picture taken by the Russian satellite, Lunik III, we now know what it looks like (Figure 2-4), and further pictures will undoubtedly give more detail. The other side looks somewhat like the side we see at full moon — with its craters and seas.

Sometimes the moon is eclipsed partly or fully. In the sun's eclipse (see page 12), the moon gets between the earth and the sun. In a lunar eclipse, the earth cuts off the sun's light from the moon.

At home take a flashlight (the sun) and shine it on a basketball (the moon). Now pass your hand (the earth) between the light and the ball. You cut off the "sun's" light and you cast a shadow on the ball; the ball, your model of a moon, is "eclipsed." Figure 2-6 is a very interesting picture of a partial eclipse of the moon over New York City. At the lower left the moon is eclipsed. Slowly it moves out of the shadow cast on it by the earth. It is, you can see, a full moon.

When the sun is shining almost straight down into a moon crater, we can see no shadows, or at least only very short ones. Down in the tropics here on our earth the shadows at noon are very short because the sun is shining

Figure 2-3.   The phases of the moon. The bottom pictures are roughly first quarter, second and third quarters, and full moon. A really full moon, with its features, is shown in Figure 2-2. Even on these photographs of the moon you can see some of the craters.

(Bausch & Lomb Optical Co.)

straight down from almost right overhead. If you look at
that big crater called Copernicus in Figure 2-7, you will see
that the shadows are short. This is because the sun is almost
directly overhead. On the other hand, in Figure 2-8, where
the daylight and darkness meet on the left-hand edge of the
crescent, the shadows are so long that they extend entirely
across a crater. They are like the long shadows on the earth
at sunset or sunrise.

Figure 2-4.   The back of the moon. It is not a very good picture, but it
is the *first* one, as photographed by cameras aboard the Russian rocket,
Lunik III. The line at the left marks the limit of what we see from the
earth. Only the numbered areas have been named.   *(Sovfoto)*

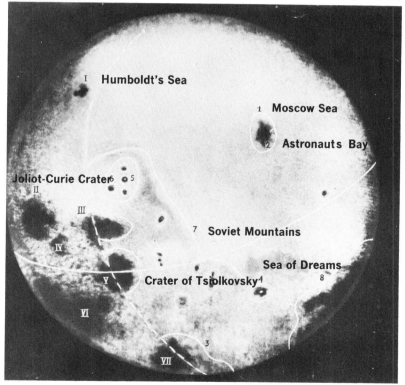

Figure 2-5.   A diagram of the Russian Lunik III. The sun's light is indicated by the direction of the three arrows. The camera opening is at (a); the solar batteries that take their energy from the sun at (b). The different knobs contain instruments that can be triggered from earth.   *(Sovfoto)*

From one full moon to the next is about 29½ days. The moon is so far from the earth — nearly a quarter of a million miles — that the journey from one full moon to the next is long and, nowadays, uneventful. To meet her new-moon, quarter-moon, and full-moon appointments, the moon has to travel over its path at the rate of over half a mile a second around the earth (Figure 2-9).

Actually, the moon doesn't truly circle the earth. The two bodies really spin about a common center. They might be likened to two dancers, arms locked, spinning around a solar

Figure 2-6.   A partial eclipse of the moon over New York. When this picture was made, the moon was photographed every fifteen minutes starting at the lower left. Slowly it came out of the shadow cast by the earth — a full moon.

(Hayden Planetarium, American Museum of Natural History)

dance floor. Since the earth is 81 times heavier than the moon, it is the anchor man in this dance. While the moon remains "facing" its heavier partner, the earth rotates on its axis more than 27 times for each time the "dancers" spin around each other.

A man on the moon would see the earth in a great hazy halo; this is due to the permanent atmosphere the earth holds. To a man on the moon the earth would appear almost motionless. And a man on the moon would be a remarkable high-jumper; he could easily jump twenty or thirty

Figure 2-7.   The big crater Copernicus. The sun is shining directly over-head; hence the shadows are short.

(Mount Wilson and Palomar Observatories)

Figure 2-8.   On the other hand, when the sun doesn't shine directly on a crater, the shadows are long enough to darken the craters and other parts of the moon completely. It is like sunset or sunrise on earth.

(Mount Wilson and Palomar Observatories)

feet, because the force of gravitation on the moon is less than that on earth. This is due to the smaller size of the moon.

If you think that the moon has a long journey to make every 29½ days, you must agree that the earth has a still harder time, for keeping always about 90 million miles from the sun, it must make the circuit of its nearly circular path every year. To accomplish this, it must move over 18 miles per second around the sun. And you, of course, move with it.

ONE MONTH (28 days)

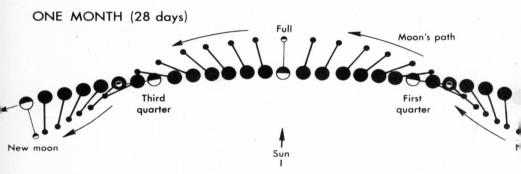

Figure 2-9.   The journey of the moon. Actually the journey from one full moon to the next takes about 29½ days. Compare the earth's position with the moon's. Both get their light from the sun. (*Drawing by Mildred Waltrip from* The Physical World *by Brinckerhoff, Cross, Watson, and Brandwein,* © *1958 by Harcourt, Brace and Company, Inc.*)

3

Mercury

From the moon, we go to the body nearest the sun —Mercury. The principles we learn about it apply to all the planets.

Far back in the remote past it was thought that there were two kinds of stars: "fixed stars" and those that move and apparently wander among the "fixed stars." The wanderers were thought to be controlled by gods. We still call many of them by the names of Greek and Roman gods, such as Mercury, Venus, Mars, Jupiter, and Saturn. What these wandering stars could be, if they were not gods and goddesses, was a mystery for thousands of years. It wasn't until the invention of the telescope, approximately three hundred and fifty years ago (about A.D. 1608), that we knew they must be huge round bodies very similar to the earth and moon and visible by reflected sunlight. Soon it was proved that this was also true of all the so-called wanderers; we now know them as planets.

Naturally, the side of the planet that is away from the sun is in darkness, just as the side of a tree that is away from the campfire is in darkness. A view from the sun would show all the planets as bright round discs, but the sun's rays light only one side at a time and the other half away from the sun must be in darkness.

In a telescope, the planets Mercury and Venus, which are between us and the sun, look like miniature moons. Sometimes we see them as thin crescents, at other times as half moons, and then again as nearly full moons.

Mercury is so small and so near the sun that it is seldom seen. Its orbit is the smallest of all the planets. Obviously, we cannot see Mercury in the daytime, so we must look for it just after sunset or just before sunrise, though, even then, twilight and clouds near the horizon make it very difficult to see.

The Greeks thought that there were two stars: one, which they called Apollo, appeared in the east just before sunrise, and the other, which they called Mercury, was seen only in the west just after sunset. When we found that these two stars were really the same planet, we gave it the name of Mercury. The Egyptians were as badly mistaken as the Greeks and gave separate names to the two appearances: Set and Horus.

Mercury is much smaller than the earth and would be an unpleasant place in which to live. It is so near the sun that the heat must be terrific, but from our point of view it has a still more serious defect; it has either no air at all or extremely little. Also, as far as we know, it always presents the same side toward the sun. It accomplishes this by slowly turning as it travels around the sun. It is much as if you were to side-step around a campfire so that you always were facing the fire.

The planet Mercury keeps the same side always toward the sun because the sun has made it rotate in that way. Several thousand millions of years ago when Mercury was young and plastic, the sun pulled it so hard by means of gravitation that it became a little warped and bulged a bit in the direction of the sun. It became just a trifle egg-shaped. Then the gravitation of the sun tended to keep one of the bulging sides (a tidal bulge) always facing it. The sun couldn't accomplish this all at once. However, through millions of years the sun, by continuously acting on these bulging sides, made Mercury spin more slowly on its axis. As the spinning on its axis grew slower, the day on Mercury grew longer and longer until finally one side was left always in darkness and the other side always in light.

Mercury is not the only body to behave in this way. As you have read in Chapter 2, if you look at the moon through a field glass, opera glass, or spyglass of any kind, you always will see the same bright mountains and the same dark plains, month after month. In this case, the powerful tidal forces of the earth have warped our satellite and made it very slightly egg-shaped.

In order to understand why Mercury has no air, we must remember that iron, wood, and even human beings are mostly empty space, but containing a number of atoms. As you might guess, in air oxygen and nitrogen have plenty of elbow room in which to dart about. Although they frequently bump into each other, they manage to develop a very considerable speed.

What we call heat is largely the degree of speed achieved by invisible particles, made up of atoms or groups of atoms. When the groups of atoms are chemically combined, we call the groups molecules. The air we breathe is full of very rapidly moving particles, made up of atoms and molecules. We can imagine air 100° below zero (Fahrenheit). Then the particles of which the air is made would be much more sluggish than they are in the ordinary air we breathe. As long as we are imagining, let us imagine the air so cold that the atoms and molecules do not move at all. That would certainly be the very coldest temperature that it would be possible to have. On the ordinary thermometer scale, this temperature would be 459.4° below zero (Fahrenheit). In the laboratory some things have been made so cold that they were only about 3° (Fahrenheit) above this absolute zero, as this complete lack of heat is called. Yet even when the temperature of a body is at absolute zero and the atoms themselves are still, it is thought that inside of them the little electrons continue running around their nuclei at their usual tremendous speed.

If a body at absolute zero were left in your room and you made no effort to keep it cold, its atoms would soon acquire increasing motion from contact with the moving atoms in the surrounding air, and in a comparatively short time they would be rushing past each other and bumping into each other with the same speed as the particles that make up this paper or your hand.

If your room were rather chilly, if its temperature were 32° (Fahrenheit), the small particles in the air you are constantly breathing would bounce from one another with an average speed of almost two miles per second. This is only the average speed. Many of the particles, whether atoms or molecules, would strike, bounce, and strike again with a speed several times greater. As you heated up your room to make yourself more comfortable, the speed would increase.

It is a curious fact that all atoms do not have the same speed when they are subjected to the same degree of heat. Oxygen, nitrogen, and water vapor, the three chief gases of our air, all behave about alike. On the other hand, helium gas, which we use in dirigibles, will bounce from one collision to another with about twice the velocity of these gases. Some helium atoms may have a speed of twenty-five miles per second.

Even at the temperature at which water freezes, a hydrogen atom has an *average* speed of more than seven miles per second. And on Mercury, the blinding sunlight is so intense that it would make even oxygen atoms, which are so much heavier than hydrogen, excitable. This excitability passes rapidly to all other atoms, and they soon are bouncing about at great speed. Because Mercury is relatively small and, therefore, has a low gravitational pull, the atoms bounce off it as soon as their speeds are in excess of two miles per second. Remember that on earth a rocket can escape from the earth only if it is shot up into the air with a velocity of about seven miles a second. On Mercury, such a rocket would need to reach a velocity of only two miles per second to leave the planet.

In any event, it was in this way that Mercury is suspected to have lost all its air, lost all the gases that from time to time were emitted by its volcanoes. Of course, there may be some gases left, but we can find no trace of them.

4

Venus

We still know very little about Venus, which travels a lonely path around the sun between the earth and Mercury. Venus is lonely from our point of view because she has no moon.

These two neighboring planets — the earth and Venus — are very nearly the same size. Venus has the inside path in going around the sun and, therefore, receives more heat.

As we watch Venus from night to night, we find she never gets very far from the sun. We must see her in the western sky just after sunset, or in the eastern sky before sunrise. On these occasions Venus is exceedingly brilliant and can frequently be seen to cast a shadow.

Like Mercury, Venus presents all the phases of the moon and for the same reason (Figure 4-1). She shines by means of reflected sunlight, so that we sometimes see her in the telescope as a thin crescent, sometimes as a half Venus, and sometimes as a nearly round bright disc like a full moon. Once in a while Venus comes directly between us and the sun. Then we see her projected against the sun as a black disc, for naturally the side toward us at that moment is perfectly dark.

Figure 4-1.   No, this is not the moon. It is Venus. Since Venus, like all the planets, gets its light from the sun, it has phases like the moon — as seen from the earth.   *(Photo by E. C. Slipher, Lowell Observatory)*

Venus is so well clothed in fleecy clouds that, as she moves over her orbit, we cannot tell how often she turns around. Some astronomers have thought that she turns around about as often as the earth does. Others have believed that Venus always presents the same side to the sun. At the Mt. Wilson Observatory, astronomers have made a very careful investigation of this subject and find that Venus certainly takes longer than ten or fifteen of our days to turn once on her axis, and she may take much longer.

In early December, 1959, Commander Malcolm Ross and Charles B. Moore went aloft in a balloon, 15 miles above the earth. In their sealed capsule, which dangled below the balloon, were the most modern instruments. And with these instruments, they discovered a highly important fact: Venus has water.

This means that life could exist, where previously no life had been expected, on the earth's nearest neighbor. Life could exist beneath the 200-mile-thick clouds that have veiled the surface of Venus from man's prying telescopes. There may be oceans on Venus. The atmosphere is rich in carbon dioxide and may also contain nitrogen. There is, at present, no evidence of sufficient amounts of oxygen to support life similar to that on earth.

Now that we have described two planets you may want to visualize their relationship in size to the earth and to each other. The table on the next page should help. You may even want to show how Mercury, Venus, Earth, and Mars are related in distance to the sun. You will need (according to the table) a balloon (which will be a model of the sun), a small grain of sand (Mercury), two peas (Earth and Venus), and an object the size of a pinhead (Mars). From the table you will see what else you will need. And you will need to use your playground to make a model that will include Mars.

Figure 4-2.   A model of the solar system.

| OBJECT | DISTANCE FROM SUN | | DIAMETER | MODEL OBJECT |
	Actual (millions of miles)	Distance of Models (in feet)	Actual (miles)	
Sun	—	—	866,000	large toy balloon
Mercury	36	82	3,100	small grain of sand
Venus	67	154	7,700	pea
Earth	93	215	8,000	pea
Mars	140	327	4,200	large pinhead
Jupiter	490	1/4 mile	89,000	orange
Saturn	890	2/5 mile	71,500	orange
Uranus	1,800	3/4 mile	32,000	plum
Neptune	2,800	1¼ miles	31,000	plum
Pluto	3,700	1½ miles	3,600(?)	pea

Our moon is about 2,000 miles in diameter and averages 240,000 miles from our earth. On the model it has a diameter of a small pinhead seven inches from the earth.

The nearest star is about the same size as the sun. Its distance from the sun is 270,000 times the earth's distance. How far from the sun would the nearest star be in the model? About 60,000,000 feet.

(From The Physical World *by Brinckerhoff et al.,* © *1958 by Harcourt, Brace and Company, Inc.)*

5

Mars

Mars must have been one of the first planets discovered by prehistoric man, for its decidedly red color and, at times, its great brilliancy make it one of the most conspicuous objects in the sky.

During modern times speculation concerning the inhabitants of Mars has been incessant. We have seen them pictured in the "movies" and described in novels. Therefore, it is with unusual interest that we examine Mars, in order to find out whether conditions are at all favorable for life in any form with which we are familiar.

Mars is farther from the sun than is the earth and receives less light and heat. It doesn't necessarily follow that Mars is colder, for you know that here on the earth we have great changes in temperature, although all places are approximately the same distance from the sun. For example, it is exceedingly hot in Death Valley in Southern California, and at the same time the neighboring mountains may be covered with ice.

The amount of air a planet has seriously affects the temperature of the surface. If there is little air, the planet is very hot in the daytime and very cold at night. On the other hand, if there is plenty of air and if the planet is reasonably near the sun, the surface will be warm, at least when it is exposed to sunlight. Air behaves much like the panes of glass in a greenhouse. It lets in the light but prevents the heat from escaping. At least the air lets most of the sunlight come down to the earth, and it holds the resulting heat long enough to make us reasonably warm.

If an atom of air in the upper parts of the Martian atmosphere has a velocity of more than three miles a second, it will probably bounce away and perhaps never return. On Mercury this so-called "velocity of escape" is only about two miles per second, while on the earth and Venus it is in the neighborhood of seven miles per second. Since Mars is larger than Mercury, it can hold its atmosphere; also, since it is smaller than the earth, its atmosphere is less dense at the surface.

Mars probably has about one-sixth as much air as we have. To us, such an amount of air would be unbearably rare; we would have as much difficulty in breathing there as we do on the tops of our highest mountains.

The most prominent feature of Mars is the appearance of the brilliantly bright polar caps. They look and behave much like the snowfields on the earth. During the Martian winter they grow large, and then during the summer they either disappear or become exceedingly small.

On the earth, in the Northern Hemisphere, the shortest day is about December 21, but our coldest weather comes a month later. In the same way, June 21 usually is our longest day in the Northern Hemisphere. However, we all know that we get our greatest heat in July. This same effect is noticed on Mars. The polar cap will have its greatest extent some time after the shortest day for that hemisphere.

Since we can measure the temperature of a furnace by analyzing its light, and since we have found the temperature of the sun, it will not seem surprising that we know the temperature of Mars. At noon on Mars during the Martian summer, the temperature is about 50° Fahrenheit. At night, however, Mars must have a degree of coldness that we can measure only in our laboratories. The white polar caps are probably 90° below zero (Fahrenheit).

In the telescope, Mars is of a red or orange color with a number of dark greenish spots of irregular shape (Figure 5-1). Also there are a vast number of minute spots, some of which are so arranged that in small telescopes they give the appearance of straight lines. These lines, often called canals, may be only optical illusions. Of course, we do not know what the rows of exceedingly faint spots are.

When the Martian spring approaches and one polar cap begins to grow smaller, a band of dark green appears on the edge of the white polar cap. Then those rows of exceedingly faint spots appear near the pole, according to Percival Lowell of the Flagstaff Observatory. As the season progresses, these apparent lines can be seen extending farther down from the pole until finally, in summer, they reach the equator. They are very, very difficult to see, and consequently there has been a considerable discussion in regard to how many there are and just where they are. Observers differ to such an extent that some claim to have seen a great many fine lines, while others claim that they have never seen any.

A germ on Mars must be able not only to endure intense cold, but it must also live on a desert and breathe very, very little oxygen. There is less than one-thirtieth as much moisture in the air of Mars as there is in the air above Pasadena,

Figure 5-1. Mars. Examine carefully A, B, C. You will see different parts of Mars in view. This is evidence that Mars rotates. Some day we may see Mars close up. Then we will know what these markings are.
(Mount Wilson and Palomar Observatories)

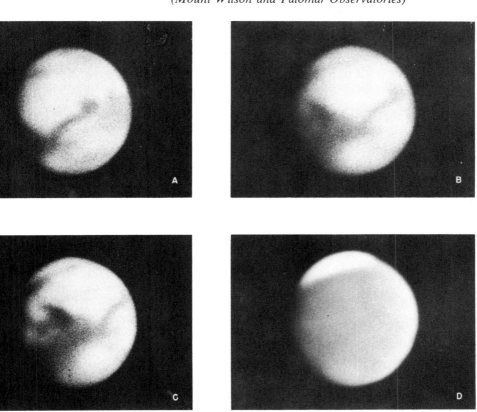

California. A luxurious vegetation depends upon moisture; it is difficult to see how Mars can boast of a flower garden. However, we generally think that green plants give free oxygen to an atmosphere by breaking up the carbon dioxide (CO_2). Therefore, we have come to believe that where we find evidence of oxygen in a planet's atmosphere, we are justified in assuming that there may be vegetation. Such seems to be the situation on Mars. But there is not as much oxygen in the Martian air as there is at sea level on the earth. When mountain climbers finally reached the top of Mt. Everest, they found it necessary to carry oxygen, for there is very little in the air at that enormous elevation. On Mars the situation is even worse, for it has been found that the Martian air contains less than two-thirds as much oxygen as we find above Mt. Everest.

While we are still on Mars, let's look beyond it. We can see its two moons, Deimos and Phobos. But beyond these moons, looking toward Jupiter, you would find a host of small planets; so small are they that some of them are no more than flying mountains (Figure 5-2). They are monstrous pieces of rock, cold and lifeless.

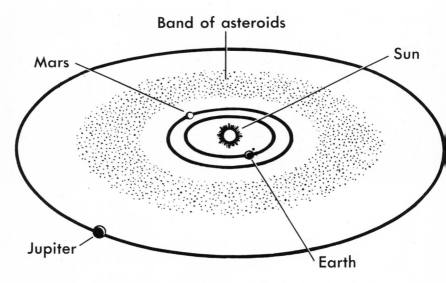

Figure 5-2.   The band of asteroids, or planetoids, between Mars and Jupiter. Their origin is still a mystery. *(Drawing by Mildred Waltrip from* The Physical World *by Brinckerhoff et al., © 1958 by Harcourt, Brace and Company, Inc.)*

The largest of these small planets, or asteroids, is Ceres, and it is only about five hundred miles in diameter. Compare it with the diameter of the earth, some fifteen times greater. So small an object as Ceres has difficulty in hanging on to any atmosphere. And if you were to visit Ceres, it couldn't very well hang on to you. You would find yourself practically weightless. And so while you might be able to jump four feet high on earth, a similar jump on Ceres would take you up several miles — till you fell back to Ceres ever so gently.

6

Jupiter

The king of the gods on Mt. Olympus took for himself the largest planet. Jupiter was his name, according to the Romans, and Jupiter still is the name of this wandering star.

The almost circular path of this planet is next beyond the orbit of Mars. When you reach Jupiter, you are getting far away from the sun — almost 500 million miles away — so that the path is very large. It takes Jupiter a long time to make the circuit, nearly twelve years.

If a spaceman should ever visit Jupiter, he would marvel at the size and beauty of this king of the planets (Figure 6-1). Next to the sun it is the largest body in the solar system, for Jupiter is almost 90,000 miles in diameter, eleven times greater than the earth's diameter. It has, therefore, about 150 times more square miles of surface than the earth. What a planet it would be to explore and map! We have only seven continents; yet there are vast stretches in nearly all of them into which no man has ever penetrated. That is particularly true of North and South America, and even parts of the United States. If the earth were as large as Jupiter, there might be 1,050 continents to explore, for there are seven continents here on the earth, and there might conceivably be 150 times as many on a planet like Earth, only as large as Jupiter. It would take thousands of years to map such a maze of continents.

If anyone lives on Jupiter, he must be as queer as any prehistoric fossil that has ever been discovered, for there is a dense atmosphere that is always full of yellow and red clouds. One great spot appeared on Jupiter during the last century and lasted many decades. It moved about as if floating in a fluid medium. It was a huge affair, much larger than

Figure 6-1.   Jupiter. Next to the sun, it is the largest body in the solar system. Notice the large spot (which is red) — larger than the continents on earth — on the upper left. And notice also one of Jupiter's satellites — one of its moons, called Ganymede — on the upper right of the photograph.   (*Mount Wilson and Palomar Observatories*)

all the seven continents of the earth. It now has nearly disappeared. We do not know what it was or what became of it.

Astronomers used to think that all this turmoil was due to heat. They thought Jupiter was still hot and had not had time to cool off. We now know that it is cold, but we do not know why it should be so different from the earth and Mars. Perhaps when Jupiter was formed, it received a combination of material that is different from that which we have in the earth. Later we will find that its great distance from the sun may have helped to give Jupiter a different assortment of rocks and liquid from that with which we are familiar.

As soon as Galileo looked at Jupiter with a telescope, he found that it had four moons. Now we know there are twelve moons, and perhaps some day we will discover more by means of very large telescopes. A curious thing was noticed about these moons as early as 1675. A Danish astronomer, Roemer (Figure 6-2), found that the eclipses of the moons as they occasionally entered the shadow of Jupiter were too early according to the predicted time when the earth was between the sun and Jupiter. Then, when the earth was on the other side of its orbit so that the sun was between it and Jupiter, the eclipses of the moons always came later than he expected. In other words, when the earth is nearest to Jupiter, the eclipses take place about eight minutes earlier than the average time of occurrence. On the other hand, when the earth is farthest from Jupiter — 180 million miles farther — the eclipses occur about eight minutes later.

This was a very puzzling situation. Why should the distance of the earth from Jupiter make the eclipses of Jupiter's moons come sometimes earlier and at other times later? Could it be possible that light takes time to travel? If so, it must take 16 minutes to cross the earth's orbit. Roemer had made an amazing discovery. At that time however, in 1675, nearly everyone thought light was instantaneous, and so they paid little attention to the Danish astronomer's findings.

The velocity of light is now determined on earth by special means as 186,284 miles per second. But Roemer's discovery stands as an amazing feat.

Figure 6-2.   Alaus Roemer (1644-1710), a Danish astronomer who was so far ahead of his time that he was not so much appreciated by his contemporaries as he was by those of following generations. There had been idle discussion as to whether light was instantaneous, as gravity is supposed to be, or whether it took time to travel. By observing the eclipses of Jupiter's satellites, Roemer proved that light required a number of minutes to cross the earth's orbit. We now know that it takes about eight minutes to come to us from the sun. However, it was some time before Roemer's demonstration was accepted.   *(Yerkes Observatory)*

7

Saturn

Next beyond Jupiter, as we travel from the sun, is the bright planet Saturn (Figure 7-1). To the Babylonians and Greeks, Saturn represented the outer limit of the solar system, for the planets that are still farther from the sun are too faint to be seen with the naked eye. These very distant planets were not discovered until after the telescope was invented, which was in comparatively recent times — about the time of the founding of Jamestown in Virginia. Saturn is a very white planet as it wanders in the heavens. Even if it has lost the prestige of the Greek god Saturn, it has retained the name. It is distinguished among its associated planets, for it carries through space some wonderful rings. Of course the ancients knew nothing of this unique feature, for the rings were not discovered until a fairly good telescope was made in 1655. Galileo saw two spots of light on each side of Saturn with his little telescope in 1610. Some years later, Saturn was in such a position that the rings were edgewise as seen from the earth. This made them invisible because of their thinness. Their disappearance puzzled the Italian astronomer, who suggested, with some amusement perhaps,

Figure 7-1.   Saturn with its rings. The rings are not solid but are made up of numerous small bodies. *(Mount Wilson and Palomar Observatories)*

that the planet was following the example of his namesake and eating his own children (Figure 7-2).

Some people think that Saturn is the most beautiful object in the heavens. A snow-white globe surrounded by equally white rings make it a mysterious as well as a fascinating planet. At first, the rings were thought to be a thin sheet of solid rock. However, it soon was realized that the gravitational forces of Saturn would cause a solid ring to break into many pieces.

The rings of Saturn we now know really consist of innumerable small bodies. There are so many of these particles, and they are so close together, that they seem to us to be a smooth white ring. Unfortunately, our telescopes are not large enough to see the separate bodies that make up the rings of Saturn. Yet we know that they are there.

J. E. Keeler of the Lick Observatory at the University of California made an examination of the light from the inner edge of the ring by means of prisms or their equivalent. Then he determined how fast the inner edge of the ring was moving. He did the same thing to the light from the outer edge of the ring and found that it was moving much more slowly. This is as it should be, if the ring consists of individual bodies that are moving around Saturn in orbits. Furthermore, the speeds found by Keeler are exactly those that the attraction of Saturn would require in accordance with the forces of gravitation.

Figure 7-2.   Another view of Saturn, which shows its rings almost edgewise. Sometimes the rings look like a thin line around the planet.
(Lick Observatory)

Of Saturn itself little is known. It is obvious that we are looking upon a very extensive atmosphere. Apparently, we see only the faint outlines of clouds or streams of clouds. Those prevailing winds called trade winds, which we find here on this earth near the equator, might present a similar appearance if they could be seen from a great distance. The belts on both Jupiter and Saturn look much like prevailing winds in their dense atmospheres.

Saturn is a large planet. It is about 70,000 miles in diameter, which is about nine times greater than the earth's diameter. This dimension makes Saturn over 700 times greater in volume. You would, therefore, expect that the planet would be approximately 700 times greater in weight. That, however, is not so, for Saturn has only about 100 times more real substance, which, if it could be placed on the earth, would be said to have weight. This means that Saturn is made of very light material, so light as to be less than three-quarters as dense as water. In the center it is undoubtedly more dense, and on the surface less dense, than water.

No molecules or atoms of Saturn's atmosphere ever wander off to visit either Uranus or Jupiter. Even if Saturn is light, and perhaps half gas and half liquid, its great size gives it tremendous attractive power. The velocity of escape is about twenty miles per second. In the intense cold of the outer layers of its atmosphere, it is very improbable that many molecules or atoms can develop such a speed.

Saturn takes nearly thirty earth years to travel once around the sun, and it has nine moons.

8

Uranus, Neptune, and Pluto

The planets Uranus and Neptune were unknown to the Babylonians and Greeks. Since they can be seen only by the aid of a telescope, they were not discovered until recently. Like Jupiter and Saturn, they are both large. These outer planets are all much bigger than the planets near the sun, such as Mars, Earth, and Venus. Also, like Jupiter and Saturn, these two planets lack that density we find so convenient when we walk on the surface of the earth. The average density of their atmosphere is only a little more than that of water. This means probably that they must be considerably denser than water at the center and, like Jupiter and Saturn, covered by a deep atmosphere.

Apparently we see only layers of clouds, floating in dense atmosphere, that rest on curious and perhaps liquid surfaces. No very brilliant sunlight gets through these clouds, for these two planets are a long distance from the center of the solar system. Uranus (Figure 8-1) is nearly 20 times farther from the sun than the earth is, and Neptune is 30 times farther. Consequently, their paths around the sun are enormously long. It takes Uranus over 80 years to make the circuit, and

Neptune over 160 years. At such great distances the sun would appear to be much smaller than it does to us, but its intense brilliance still gives a fair amount of light. Daylight on Uranus is equal to about 1,500 full moons here on the earth. Sunlight on Pluto has the intensity of about 400 times that of our moon as seen from this earth.

Uranus was discovered in 1781 by Sir William Herschel with one of his telescopes. Neptune, however, made our acquaintance as a known astronomical body in a much more romantic manner.

For some time it had been known that no one could predict just where Uranus was going to be among the planets. It

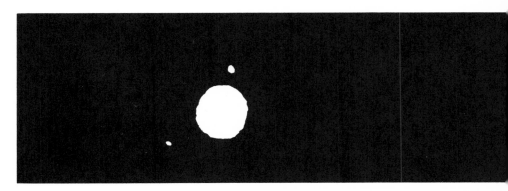

Figure 8-1.   Uranus — one of the larger planets — with two of its satellites. As yet we can't see many details of this planet; it is too far off.

(Yerkes Observatory)

didn't behave as it would behave if influenced only by the sun, Jupiter, and Saturn. It was, therefore, suspected that there might be another planet beyond Uranus. Perhaps the attraction of this unknown planet was causing Uranus to diverge a little from its predicted path.

Leverrier, a French astronomer, undertook to locate this unknown planet (Figure 8-2). His problem was to determine at what place in the solar system such a planet would have this disturbing effect upon Uranus. Having no observatory at his disposal, in 1846 he sent the following message to the German astronomer Galle at the observatory at Berlin: "Direct your telescope to a point on the ecliptic in the constellation of Aquarius, in longitude 326° and you will find within a degree of that place a new planet, looking like a star of about the ninth magnitude, and having a perceptible disk."* The planet was promptly found by Galle within nine-tenths of a degree of the predicted place.

In the meanwhile, another astronomer, J. C. Adams of England, also had solved the problem and located the unknown planet. Like Leverrier, Adams had no telescope with which to verify his figures. He, therefore, notified Challis, at the astronomical observatory of Cambridge University. After some delay Challis began to observe the stars in the neighborhood of the predicted place in order to find if any star was changing its position. Before the Cambridge astronomer had completed this survey, the news arrived of the discovery by Galle at Berlin.

It was later discovered that Challis at Cambridge had actually observed Neptune twice in his survey but did not recognize it as a planet. The German astronomer Galle had a great advantage, for he had a new chart of the faint stars in that neighborhood. When he compared the chart with the sky, he very soon found a star that was not recorded. A few hours' observation showed that this unmapped star was moving and was, indeed, the predicted planet, later called Neptune (Figure 8-3).

Neither Leverrier nor Adams knew that the other was

* From *Astronomy*, by Russell, Dugan, Stuart; Ginn and Company, publishers.

Figure 8-2.   Urbain Jean Joseph Leverrier (1811-1877), one of France's most illustrious astronomers. He was born at St. Leo in Normandy and educated in the Ecole Polytechnique. At the suggestion of Arago, the Director of the Paris Observatory, Leverrier studied the irregular motions of Uranus. He concluded there was an unknown planet causing the trouble. Galle, of the Berlin Observatory, in 1846 discovered this planet, afterward called Neptune, in almost the exact place predicted by Leverrier. In 1854, Leverrier was made Director of the Paris Observatory and was twice given a gold medal by the Royal Astronomical Society of Great Britain.   *(French Press and Information Service)*

trying to solve this problem. It was a situation that was similar to the formulation of some of the principles of evolution, independently, by both Darwin and Wallace.

Even after the discovery of Neptune, Uranus failed to occupy its predicted position with all the accuracy that was expected of it. Again astronomers suspected that another planet beyond Neptune was causing these apparent irregularities. Many years ago Percival Lowell began a long series of computations to find the probable position of a distant planet that might be causing Uranus to deviate slightly from its predicted path. In 1929, the Lawrence Lowell telescope was installed at the Lowell Observatory at Flagstaff, Arizona, and a set of photographs was made of the stars in the region where this unknown planet was supposed to be.

The method used was to compare two photographs taken at different dates and search for some object that had changed its place by even a very small amount. This work was done by means of a microscope. Early in 1930, a faint light was found on the photographic plates that moved

Figure 8-3. Neptune and its satellite. It is one of the farthermost planets; one more lies beyond it. (*Yerkes Observatory*)

Figure 8-4.   Pluto, the outermost planet. The two photographs show its motion in twenty-four hours. *(Mount Wilson and Palomar Observatories)*

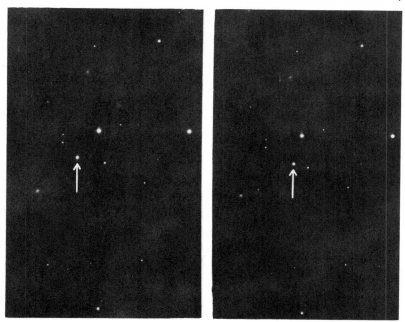

among the stars at about the speed a planet beyond Neptune would be expected to have, and not far from the place predicted by Percival Lowell. It proved to be a ninth planet, about 40 times as far from the sun as the earth is and traveling in an oval orbit around the sun in about 250 years (Figure 8-4). At this rate it takes about four months to travel through the sky a distance corresponding to the apparent diameter of the moon. The director of the Lowell Observatory gave the name Pluto to this new and outermost of the major planets.

Now that you have made the acquaintance of the earth's neighbors — the members of the solar system — you may want to re-examine Figure 1-3 to fix their positions in mind.

And you may want to study the table below, which sum-
marizes certain facts about them. Notice that we still don't
know with any exactitude even elementary facts about Pluto.
It makes us realize how little we know and how much remains to be discovered.

Figure 8-5.   Relative Sizes of the Sun, Moon, and Planets

DISTANCES from Earth in Miles*		SIX PLANETS HAVE MOONS**	
The moon	240,000	The earth has	1
Venus	26,000,000	Mars	2
Mars	48,000,000	Neptune	2
Mercury	57,000,000	Uranus	5
The sun	93,000,000	Saturn	9
Jupiter	390,000,000	Jupiter	12
Saturn	793,000,000		—
Uranus	1,690,000,000	Total	31
Neptune	2,700,000,000		
Pluto	3,573,000,000		

*If you wanted to travel to these places, the distances would be much greater because a space rocket cannot travel in a straight line.

**Our moon is 2,160 miles in diameter. The smallest, Mars's moon Deimos, is 5 miles in diameter. The largest, Jupiter's moon Ganymede, is 3,200 miles in diameter.

(*Drawing by Mildred Waltrip from* You and Science *by Brandwein et al., copyright, 1950, 1952, 1955 by Harcourt, Brace and Company, Inc.*)

Mercury

Venus

Earth   moon

Mars

SUN

Jupiter

Saturn

Uranus

Neptune

Pluto

9

What Holds Them Together?

Have you ever wondered what keeps the earth in its orbit around the sun? What keeps the other planets moving around the sun? The laws of falling bodies are very interesting to everyone, especially to someone on an icy path. People had only hazy ideas on this subject until Galileo examined how fast balls would fall from a high tower (Figure 9-1). It was about three hundred years ago that the famous Italian scientist found that a piece of wood would fall from the top of the tower to the ground in about the same time as a piece of iron. A ten-pound piece of lead will fall as fast as a one-pound piece of the same metal, except for a very slight effect due to the resistance of the air. You know that the faster you go in an automobile, the greater is the pressure of the wind against the windows. The air has the same effect upon a falling body; it tends very slightly to slow up its motion.

Everything falls toward the center of the earth if it is given a chance. The speed of the fall has nothing to do with the material of which the thing is made.

There is a mysterious force that makes an apple fall from

a tree and that also compels the moon to revolve around the earth. Sir Isaac Newton called this force "gravity" and said that it behaved as if the earth attracted the apple and the moon. We do not know what this thing called gravity is. Newton was the first to tell us how it behaves, and Einstein was the latest to describe it, and in still greater detail. We say that because of gravitation the earth attracts a falling apple, or that the sun attracts the earth and thereby compels the earth to revolve around it. We do not mean that the earth and sun act like magnets. We merely mean that there is a mysterious force associated with the earth and sun and all bodies that makes them behave as if they were attracting each other. For instance, meteors are attracted to the earth once they come within the pull of the earth's gravitational force. A comet is acted upon by the sun's tremendous gravitational pull.

The apparent attraction of the earth is very strong, as you well know when you try to jump over a fence. It is fortunate for us that it is, for otherwise we might slip off the earth entirely and find ourselves floating around in space and having great difficulty in breathing.

The longer gravity acts on a ball that is free to fall, the faster the ball will go. A rock dropped from the Empire State Building will fall 16 feet by the end of the first second. It keeps on increasing its speed and at the end of that first second attains a velocity, or a rate of speed, of 32 feet per second.

The automobile has made us familiar with the word "rate," for we all know what it meant by "the car went at the rate of 22 miles per hour." This statement of course means that the car went so fast that if it continued at that rate of speed for a whole hour (3,600 seconds), it would

Figure 9-1. Galileo Galilei (1564-1642), Italy's most distinguished physicist and astronomer. It was in Pisa, the town in which he was born, that Galileo made his most famous observations. Even if the tower of Pisa had not leaned because of a defective foundation, it would have been famous, for Galileo from this tower proved that all bodies fall with equal velocity regardless of their weight. It is interesting to find that as late as 1597, over fifty years after the death of Copernicus, Galileo wrote to Kepler and said that while he believed the sun was the center of the solar system, he dared not make his belief public more from fear of ridicule than from fear of persecution. Galileo was the first, as far as we know, to examine the stars with the newly invented telescope. He discovered that there were mountains on the moon, that four satellites revolve around Jupiter, that Venus presents phases like the moon, that the Milky Way is not a smooth band of light but consists of innumerable stars, and that there are sometimes spots on the sun.   *(Yerkes Observatory)*

travel a distance of 22 miles (116,160 feet). If a car went 116,160 feet in 3,600 seconds, then it would go a little over 32 feet in one second, or its speed would be at the rate of 32 feet per second.

By an interesting and very simple method the distance a rock will fall at the end of any number of seconds can be determined. For a few seconds these distances are as follows:

Number of Seconds	Total Distance Fallen
1	16 feet
2	64 feet
3	144 feet
4	256 feet
5	400 feet
6	576 feet

You can sometimes get an approximate idea of the height of a cliff by dropping a rock and noting the number of seconds it takes to fall. If it takes three seconds, the height is about 150 feet. If you were to fall from a second-story window, it would take you about one second to reach the ground, and when you reached it, you would be going at about 22 miles per hour.

We know how gravity behaves, but we do not know what this mysterious thing is. Its effect varies with distance just as light does. If a body is moved twice as far away from the earth as it had been, it will be attracted with only one-quarter the force; if three times farther off, one-ninth, and so forth. The moon is 60 times as far from the center of the earth as we are. It is, therefore, affected by the earth with only 1/3600 as much force. Instead of falling toward the earth 16 feet at the end of one second, it will fall only one thirty-six-hundredth as much, or five one-hundredths of one inch (0.05 inches). However, the moon is moving through space at a very considerable rate, and the combination of falling toward the earth and also trying to keep on a straight path through space makes it go around the earth in an oval curve called an ellipse. This path is the moon's orbit.

You probably are wondering why the moon should try to go through space in a straight line. If you do ask this question, it will not be an easy one to answer. A long time ago the great English mathematician Sir Isaac Newton developed the idea that if a body is once given a push in space, it will go in a straight line forever, unless something comes along to move it to one side. Most astronomers agree that it was only a few thousand million years ago that the moon began to revolve around the earth in such a way that it never hits the earth and never flies off in a straight line.

In the same way the earth is going around the sun in an ellipse and takes one year to make the journey.

Primitive man thought that this motion was reversed. To him the earth was standing still and the sun was going around it. Since he also thought the earth was flat, he had considerable difficulty in imagining what happened to the sun when it set in the west. Some thought it was carried in a chariot through passages under the earth so that it could rise again in the east. Some of the ancient Greeks were very wise. Pythagoras claimed the earth was round. Aristarchus, according to Archimedes, announced that the earth revolved around the sun. Eratosthenes measured the earth's diameter. Unfortunately for us, the work of another Greek, Ptolemy, was used by the Europeans during the Dark Ages. Ptolemy thought the earth stood still and was the very center of the universe. For more than a thousand years our

European ancestors entertained this old notion. It was not until about four hundred years ago that an astronomer in Poland, Copernicus, announced that the earth and all the other planets went around the sun.

Still men were very much puzzled. Why did the earth go around the sun in that peculiar path called an ellipse? They thought that there must be some kind of spirit animal that guided the planets around the sun. They even went so far as to think of these spirit animals as being shaped somewhat like whales.

Finally, Sir Isaac Newton of England, about three hundred years ago, proved that gravity applies to all things, not only on the earth but in the heavens. He showed that as a result of the sun's apparent attractive power, the planets must go in paths that are ellipses (Figure 9-2).

What is gravity? The answer to that question is still unknown.

As far as we know, the force of gravitation extends to the most remote star in the sky. Of course, at such inconceivable distances, the effect of one star upon another is exeedingly slight. On the other hand, there is an unlimited time during which this effect can be exerted. When you start to pull any heavy load, you know it moves extremely slowly at first, but the longer you pull, the faster it goes, until finally it is moving at a reasonable speed. Stars behave in this same way. And so do the tremendous groups of stars called galaxies, about which you will read later.

It is strange that a star, a mere speck of light to us, invisible perhaps to the naked eye and barely visible in the most powerful telescope, can have a very great effect. However, each speck of light is really as large and about as fiery-hot as our sun. Many of them are vastly larger and hotter.

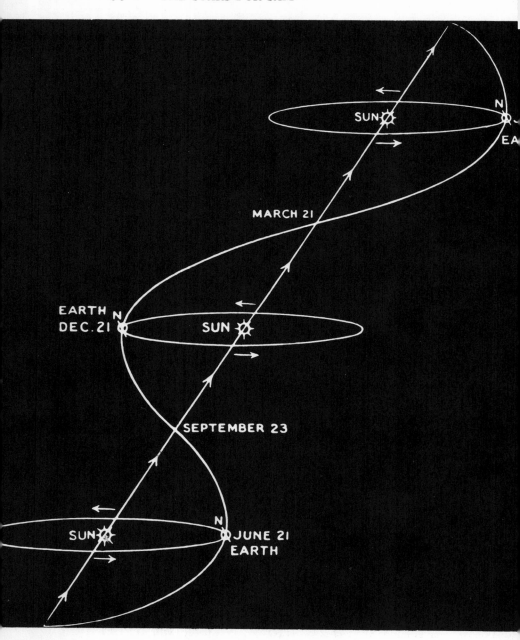

Compared with the earth, the sun is a giant. Our earth seems large to us — eight thousand miles in diameter, if we go straight through to China. Our sun, on the other hand, is more than 864,000 miles in diameter, over one hundred times greater. Its apparent attractive power, its gravitational force, is so great that a sun-man, who wanted to spend one second in falling, would be obliged to jump out of a window on the thirtieth floor, instead of a second-story window on this earth. When this sun-man landed on the surface of the sun after his one second's fall, he would be going over 600 miles per hour. Such is the size and apparent attractive force of the sun, where a body falls, not 16 feet, but 444 feet during the first second.

Figure 9-2.   The sun moves. The earth moves around the sun. The moon moves around the earth. They are all held to each other by the force of gravitation. So as the sun moves, the earth moves around it in an ellipse.

10

Visitors to Our Solar System—Meteors

At Cone Butte, in Arizona, there is a huge hole in the earth — four-fifths of a mile across and nearly 600 feet deep. The rock on the edge has been jammed up into a lofty ridge 150 feet above the surrounding level. This vast cavity is not the crest of a volcano or the bed of a sunken lake. It is the hole made by a huge meteorite, or a group of meteorites, that several thousand years ago struck the country we now call Arizona (Figure 10-1). Only tribes of Indians roamed over the plains in those days, so we do not know what happened when this celestial cannonball struck.

We can guess, however, that if there were people in that country, all of them within hundreds of miles must have thought there was an earthquake. With the shaking of the ground, there must have been a blinding flash of light. The heat was terrific, so that as far as the horizon all life, both plant and animal, must have been destroyed. Even today the rocks on the sides of this hole are burnt and crumbled (Figure 10-2).

There have been other displays of celestial fireworks in which some shooting stars struck the earth. When this hap-

Figure 10-1. The crater in Arizona. Compare it with craters on the moon. We know the crater in Arizona was caused by a meteorite. What might have been the cause of the craters on the moon?

(Trans World Airlines, Inc.)

pens, we call them meteorites, and when we see them in the sky and they do not strike the earth, we call them meteors.

In 1908, Siberia was bombarded by scores of meteorites both great and small. Fortunately for human life, this group of meteorites struck Siberia in a very remote region. As far as we know, only trees and animals were destroyed by the withering blast. A Russian expedition in 1927 described what had happened. They stated that there had been a great

Figure 10-2.   Rocks on the side of the crater in Arizona. The meteorite had tremendous force.   *(U. S. Geological Survey)*

forest that extended for fifteen miles around the spot where the meteorites struck the land.

"The trees are now all bare without bark or limbs and almost all lie on the ground with their tops turned away from the center of the spot, thus giving a sort of fan effect which is plainly visible from the tops of some of the surrounding mountains. Here and there some tree trunks still stand and in a few isolated and very sheltered spots, some are still living. But the region in general is now most desolate.

"All the vegetation shows the effect of uniform and continuous scorching, which does not in the least resemble the consequences of a forest fire. The scorching is visible on the moss and bushes as well as the trees and some signs of it appear as far as six to ten miles from the center."

The central area is covered with innumerable craters, which vary from one yard to fifty yards in diameter. An eyewitness, S. B. Seminov, described the event, although he was sixty miles from the place where the meteorites struck the earth.

"About 8 o'clock in the morning, I had been sitting on the porch with my face to the north and at this moment in the northwest direction appeared a kind of fire which produced such a heat that I could not stand it. . . . And this over-heated miracle, I guess, had a size of at least a mile. But the fire did not last long. I had only time to lift my eyes and it disappeared. Then it became dark and then followed an explosion which threw me down from the porch about six feet or more . . . but I heard a sound as if all houses would tremble and move away. Many windows were broken, a large strip of ground was torn away and at the warehouse the iron bolt was broken. . . ."*

Nearly every museum has some of these meteorites — these strange visitors — in captivity. We know that they are made of rock or iron and that some weigh only a few pounds and others many tons (Figures 10-3 and 10-4). But exactly what are these meteorites that have bombarded the earth and where do they come from?

* "The Great Siberian Meteorite," by Charles P. Oliver, University of Virginia, *Scientific American*, July, 1928.

Figure 10-3.   A polished section of a small meteorite from Kansas.
(American Meteorite Museum)

There are millions and millions of meteors in the neighborhood of the sun and earth. They are moving around the sun very much as the earth does. Since they are cold, they shine only by the light of the sun. They are so small, however, that the amount of reflected sunlight is insufficient to enable us to see them. We can see the moon because that body is so much larger, although it shines only by reflected light from the sun. Therefore, shooting stars are for the most part invisible until they enter our atmosphere; and millions of them enter every day.

These shooting stars rain down upon our atmosphere in much the way pellets of ice fall upon your car as you drive through a sleet storm. Compared with your car, the earth gets more than its share of meteorites. Imagine all the iron of your car to be very much magnetized so that it would attract

Figure 10-4. A large meteorite at the American Museum of Natural History. We do not know the size of the original meteors from which the meteorites in Figures 10-3 and 10-4 came.
(Hayden Planetarium, American Museum of Natural History)

a nail from a considerable distance. Then let us imagine that instead of little pellets of ice you found little pellets of iron raining down through the air. Under these conditions you would expect your car to be hit many more times per second than it was during the sleet storm.

The earth gathers millions of these small particles of rock and iron moving around the sun in various paths. Its force of gravitation draws some to one side and forces them to fall into the earth's atmosphere. They plunge into the air at tremendous speed, sometimes nearly forty miles per second. The friction with the air is so great that they become not only hot, but white hot. Therefore, we see their trail of glowing gases.

If they were alive, they wouldn't realize how fast they

were going. They would merely think that they had been struck by a furious wind, which was first heating and then actually blowing off all the rough edges on their surfaces. We don't always know how fast we are going until we hit something. For example, the earth is moving around the sun at the rate of more than 60 thousand miles per hour, and yet in our daily experience we think of the earth as standing still. As a meteor moves through space, he might be as ignorant as we have been in the past. He would see the sun, moon, Venus, Mars, and Jupiter, and an occasional comet, moving past him and around him in curious paths. He would probably consider that he was the center of the whole universe, which had been created for his amusement.

Suddenly he has a new sensation. He finds a strange mixture of gases called air rushing over his surfaces at the rate of more than 60 thousand miles per hour. Without knowing it, he has plunged into the earth's atmosphere. We find it difficult to stand erect against a wind that is blowing only 60 miles an hour. Therefore, it is not hard to imagine that the rough edges of our wandering meteor first become hot, then white-hot, and then are torn off entirely.

A meteor spends a fairly active life in the few seconds it exists as an incandescent body in our atmosphere before it strikes the solid earth. Fortunately for us, in most cases the minute particles called shooting stars are worn completely away before they reach the surface of the earth. Occasionally, some big fellow gets down to the land. Often such a meteorite will explode, or apparently do so, making a loud report that sounds like a distant clap of thunder.

11

Visitors to Our Solar System — Comets and "Meteor Showers"

In all ages comets have been mysteries to mankind. Like most unexplained things, they usually were associated with evil spirits. People used to think that comets brought pestilence, war, and death. While we have ceased to fear comets, we find many of their queer ways quite difficult to understand (Figure 11-1). Most comets are faint and are seen only by means of a telescope. They usually are little round patches of light, like a bit of luminous cloud. On the other hand, some comets are wonderful objects with a bright head and long graceful tail.

Whether large or small, they all move around the sun. Their paths generally are very elongated ellipses and are so long that it sometimes takes a comet hundreds of years to travel once around the sun. One comet, which visited us in 1914, requires 24 million years to make one journey around the sun. This comet was named after its discoverer, and is called Delavan's comet. Its previous visit to the earth was in the Oligocene Period, when man was not yet on earth and horses were small, with three toes in place of a hoof. When

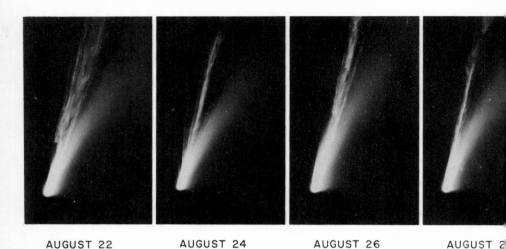

AUGUST 22   AUGUST 24   AUGUST 26   AUGUST 2

1957

Figure 11-1.   Four views of the Mrkos comet. In the photograph you can
see clearly the difference between the comet's bright head and the tail,
which becomes hazier in the parts away from the comet's head. Now
study the diagram in Figure 11-2.

(Mount Wilson and Palomar Observatories)

this comet is farthest from the sun, it is outside the solar system and about halfway to the nearest fixed star.

Some scientists believe that the head of a comet consists
of a swarm of millions of particles, possibly consisting of
small rocky bits, dust, and gases. There is some thought that
these gases are frozen in spongy masses. As the comet approaches the sun, the gas is in part set free by the action of
sunlight. Then it is illuminated by the sunlight and, in some
unknown way, also shines by its own light. It is this atmosphere of luminous gas that makes the comet's head look like
a small cloud.

Sunlight has set free many of the imprisoned atoms of
gas. As if it were at once dissatisfied with its work, it proceeds to drive these atoms off into the interminable distances

of interstellar space. All light has a certain power to repel, and thus it tends to drive minute particles in the direction in which it is traveling. It is a very slight force, so slight that a particle must be so small as to be invisible to the eye to be much affected. However, when the particles are small and when the light comes from an intensely hot body like the sun, this repulsive force can be very considerable.

The luminous gas, liberated by the sunlight and then driven away like smoke, makes the beautiful comet's tail. Naturally, as the comet goes around the sun, the tail always points away from that central source of intense light (Figure 11-2).

The solid particles, which make the head of the comet,

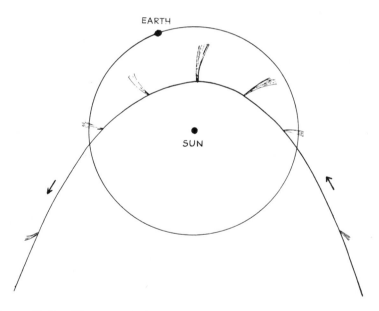

Figure 11-2.   Diagram of the path of a comet around the sun. Notice how the "head" of the comet keeps its orbit while the tail of thin gas moves away as if repelled by the sun's light.   *(Yerkes Observatory)*

probably are very small. Perhaps most of them are smaller than ordinary marbles. They move through space much like a swarm of bees. It is only when they come near the sun that the gas held by these particles is liberated and then driven away by the repelling power of sunlight.

When this swarm of particles comes near the sun, the swarm tends to spread out. In the course of ages, after many journeys near the sun, most swarms are elongated to such an extent as to become invisible. "The brilliant comet which used to visit us regularly every few years has disappeared," people say. Then as the elongation continues, the millions of particles become nearly uniformly distributed throughout their orbit. Unless interfered with by some planet, they will continue to stream around the sun for perhaps millions of years.

Such a stream — a disintegrated comet — is invisible to us unless the earth in its travels happens to plunge into it. When this occurs, we have a "shower of meteors."

The most remarkable of these showers occurred on November 13, 1833. Eyewitnesses said there were so many meteors that it seemed as if all the stars were falling. Probably several million meteors may have entered the earth's atmosphere on that occasion.

Imagine that you are walking from one large building to another during a severe hailstorm. The buildings are separated by a narrow alley. As you run from one building to another, you are pelted by the hailstones. Naturally, the hailstones hit you from only one direction, that is, the direction from which the wind is blowing. In 1833, the earth, at the rate of almost twenty miles per second, dashed through a stream of meteors, which perhaps in size were not so very different from hailstones. During the earth's brief exposure to this bombardment, its atmosphere must have been struck several million times. Yet not once, as far as we know, did one of these meteors get entirely through the air and reach the surface of the earth to become a meteorite. So great was their speed and so small was each meteor that they were entirely burnt and turned into gas and luminous dust by friction with the air.

During its journey around the sun, the earth crosses over five hundred such streams. With a few exceptions they are very feeble and the meteors are so far apart that only experts can tell that a shower is taking place.

In a first-class shower it is obvious that the meteors appear to come from a single point in the sky. In 1833, and again in 1866, this point was in the constellation of the Lion. Of course, in reality, the meteors are traveling through space in parallel lines. If they appear to come from a point, it is an illusion. A straight railroad track gives you the same illusion. The tracks appear to meet in the distance; yet you know that they are parallel lines.

The earth doesn't always encounter a swarm of shooting stars every time it crosses one of these orbits in its annual trip around the sun. Sometimes the old original comet has not been evenly distributed throughout its orbit, and we then encounter many shooting stars on one occasion and few on another. It is much like crossing that narrow alley between those large buildings. If we made the circuit of those buildings once a week and crossed that alley, we would not always encounter a hailstorm. Some hailstorms would pass down the alley, either before or after we crossed. On the other hand, one hailstorm might appear at regular intervals, so that we would become pelted with ice at every third crossing.

Harlow Shapley of the Harvard Observatory has estimated that 1,000 million of these tiny meteors enter our air every day and thereby meet with a sudden and fiery end to their existence. Yet most of them cannot be assigned to any comet we can see. Perhaps these are the separate remains of comets that have broken up.

Figure 11-3.   A remarkable photograph of the head of Halley's comet seen May 8, 1910. It will be around again in 1986; Halley's comet visits us every 76 years.   (Mount Wilson and Palomar Observatories)

Then there are large meteors that eventually reach the earth. It was one of these, in this case made mostly of iron, that fell from the sky and became the meteorite that hollowed out that crater four-fifths of a mile wide in Arizona (Figure 10-1). They also, as far as we know, have no connection with comets. Fortunately for us, these big fellows are few and far between.

Comets have a regular orbit, visiting us at predictable times. Halley's comet (Figure 11-3), the most famous, appears every 76 years. It made its last visit in May, 1910.

12

What Makes Them Up?

You now have an idea — a beginning idea, of course — of what keeps the planets together. The principle of gravitation is universal; it works on apples, on planets, and on stars. Now let us see if there is something unifying about the make-up of planets and stars. After all, the planets had a common origin — the sun, a star.

Suppose you were in a rocket moving away from the earth. What might you see as you looked back? Perhaps you would see the earth as in Figure 12-1. If Columbus could have seen the earth this way, he would have had easy proof that it was a sphere — not flat.

Suppose now you returned to earth; of course, you would land on special landing stations in the desert. What would the desert look like a hundred miles up — even two miles up? Like a flat, solid sheet. Yet you know the surface of the desert is made up of tiny sand grains. Therefore, the flat, apparently solid sheet is made up of great numbers of tiny particles.

Those wonderful Greeks had made a good guess about the make-up of things around them. Democritus thought that if one could take a knife and divide up solid material, like a sheet of metal, one would eventually come to the smallest part, a very tiny particle indeed that still had the properties of the metal.

If you could divide up a sheet of iron, you would eventually come to an invisible particle, the smallest part of the sheet of iron that was still iron. This is an *atom* of iron.

Groups of one kind of atom make up an element. Therefore, the element iron is made up of atoms of iron; gold is made up of atoms of gold and only atoms of gold. Air is made up largely of a mixture of atoms of several elements, such as oxygen and nitrogen. Chemists and physicists now

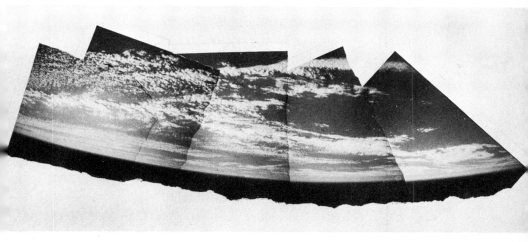

Figure 12-1. A rocket's view of the earth. What proof does this offer you that the earth is a sphere?   *(Official U. S. Navy Photograph)*

have discovered 102 elements. And what is most exciting, ten of these have been made in the laboratory by scientists.

The meteorites shown in Figures 10-3 and 10-4 are made up mostly of iron, with some amounts of the elements nickel and cobalt.

Sometimes several atoms will combine to make a very useful but more complex substance. When two atoms of hydrogen combine with one atom of oxygen, a compound substance is made that we call water. Atoms of carbon, hydrogen, and oxygen, when combined in certain proportions, make sugar. If the same atoms are combined in slightly different proportions, they make alcohol. Such little groups of atoms are called molecules. A molecule of water, for example, consists of two atoms of hydrogen and one atom of oxygen.

Until recently no one knew what these atoms would look like if you could examine them through that imaginary and powerful microscope. It was probably generally assumed that they were round balls, absolutely indivisible, the very foundation of all real substance.

They were not supposed to be packed solidly together like a barrel of pebbles. Scientists knew there must be space between them even in the densest of bodies, such as a bar of lead. They realized that the molecules moved around among themselves. Even in ice there is space between the molecules, and there is considerable movement. When ice melts and becomes water, there is a great deal of movement among the molecules. Finally, when you heat the water so much that it turns into steam, the molecules at once jump far apart and dart around at a very high speed. In fact, they try so hard to get away from each other that they sometimes burst the boiler that is holding them.

For a long while, then, we have been realizing that all things are not so solid as they appear to be. Rocks, wood, and animals are like that distant smooth band of green that proves to be a forest of trees, or the desert, which is something like a smooth sheet. To some extent, each piece of rock is something like a swarm of bees. At a distance the bees look like a faint cloud and move as a whole, very much as a cloud does. Perhaps another swarm of bees of a different kind might shy away from them, much as two balls would bounce away from each other.

When the bees have gathered on a tree and are clustered close together, it is possible to pick up a handful of them and handle them somewhat as you would a snowball.

To an enormous giant who could see immense distances but who was almost blind to minute things near at hand, this swarm of bees would look like a solid ball. A swarm of bees would look to him like smoke. If you told him that the "ball" was really a mass of little bodies that were moving among themselves and that there was a good deal of space between them, he would laugh at you and say you had a vivid imagination. Then, if you told him that the smoke was really a swarm of individual bees moving very rapidly and that there was a great deal of space around each bee, he would be more surprised than ever.

It would probably be true that in that ball there was more empty space than there was actual bee-substance, for their wings and legs kept them from packing very closely. In other words, that ball the giant saw was perhaps four-fifths empty space and only one-fifth real bee-substance. The smoke or swarm may have been ninety-nine-hundredths empty space and only one-hundredth bee-substance.

It has taken chemists and physicists many years to learn about atoms and the enormous amount of empty space in all things.

In 1911, Sir Ernest Rutherford of England discovered the atom was not so simple after all. He proved it was made of many even more minute particles. Later, Niels Bohr of

Denmark likened diagrams of an atom to a very tiny solar system. In the center of each atom is a nucleus, which consists of protons and neutrons. Around this nucleus revolve electrons. How they revolve is not quite known — but for our purposes we might think of electrons revolving around the nucleus like the planets around the sun.

Now we know that all matter on all planets — all substance — consists of electrons, neutrons, and protons. The difference between copper and lead or between one element and another is in the number of protons. Neutrons add to the weight of the atoms; neutrons and protons together make up its atomic weight. Electrons weigh very little and do not add much to the weight of an atom.

The simplest of all elements is hydrogen gas, in which one electron revolves around a nucleus (Figure 12-2). It is as if the solar system consisted of just the sun and Mercury. Next in complexity comes helium — the nonexplosive gas used in dirigibles. Two electrons revolve around the nucleus

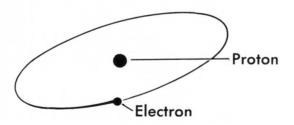

Ordinary hydrogen

Figure 12-2.   A diagram of an atom of hydrogen. One electron revolves around the proton. *(Drawing by Mildred Waltrip from* The Physical World *by Brinckerhoff et al., © 1958 by Harcourt, Brace and Company, Inc.)*

(Figure 12-3). The sun and the planets Mercury and Venus represent this miniature solar system. The familiar element carbon, of which coal and diamonds are made, has six electrons that revolve around the nucleus. The nucleus of carbon has six protons and six neutrons (Figure 12-4). Nitrogen has seven electrons revolving around its nucleus, oxygen eight, iron twenty-six, silver forty-seven, gold seventy-nine, and finally uranium, the most complicated element of those that occur naturally, has ninety-two electrons revolving in orbits around its very heavy nucleus. The nucleus of uranium has 92 protons and 146 neutrons.

Our fathers and our grandfathers realized that no substance could be absolutely solid, that the atoms of which it consisted must have space in which to move. Never for a moment did they suspect the amount of space that really exists. Not only were those atoms farther apart than our ancestors estimated, but each atom, instead of being a small round ball, now is found to be something like a little solar

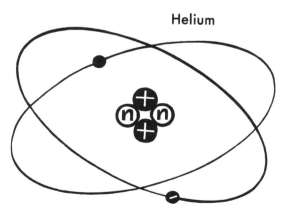

Figure 12-3.   A diagram of an atom of helium. In the nucleus are two protons, and two neutrons. How many electrons revolve around the nucleus? *(Drawing by Mildred Waltrip from* The Physical World *by Brinckerhoff et al., © 1958 by Harcourt, Brace and Company, Inc.)*

Figure 12-4.   A diagram of an atom of carbon. How many electrons revolve around its nucleus? *(Drawing by Mildred Waltrip from* The Physical World *by Brinckerhoff et al.,* © *1958 by Harcourt, Brace and Company, Inc.)*

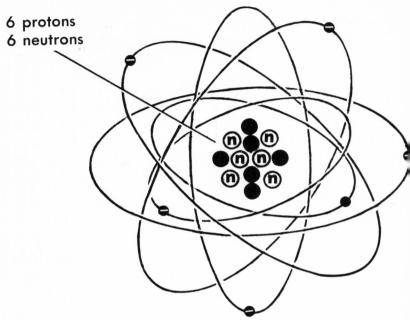

6 protons
6 neutrons

system, or perhaps like a little group of waves revolving around each other in some mysterious fashion. We certainly don't know what protons, neutrons, and electrons look like. These electrons and protons are so minute that, compared with their size, they are a long way apart. Yet to us they are all so close together that they cannot be separated with a microscope.

The distance across the nearly circular path of a typical electron is about 50 thousand times greater than the electron's own diameter. If you wanted to make a large model of an atom, you might choose a golf ball to represent an electron. Then the nucleus must be about half a mile away.

It certainly would be true that such an atom would consist almost entirely of empty space. Of course, the proportion of space to substance would be the same whether your model were a mile in diameter or microscopically small.

Why don't we sink into the rock upon which we are sitting? How can such an overwhelming proportion of empty space be as hard as iron? The answer is we, ourselves, are also merely airy nothingness. We don't sink into the rock any more than those swarms of bees would mix together. The electrons, revolving around the nucleus with incredible speed, are the centers of powerful and largely unknown forces. From time to time, as you read about new explorations, you can change your description of the atom, for probably each decade will bring your opinion nearer and nearer to the truth.

So everything about you is made up of atoms. Later on you will learn that the elements found on the earth are found in other planets through studies made by a special instrument — the spectroscope.

You will also learn, as you go on to study science, that the sun gets its tremendous energy by changing hydrogen into helium. You have already heard about the hydrogen bomb. It also develops its tremendous energy by changing hydrogen into helium. Put very simply, the basis of the process is to encourage atoms of hydrogen — four of them — to *fuse*. In fusing, they form helium, and in the process of fusion some of the atomic material is changed into energy — the force of the bomb (Figure 12-5a).

Well, the sun is a huge helium factory. In it, hydrogen atoms fuse to form helium — and in the process, the sun gives off its energy, heat, and light (Figure 12-5b). This is the energy on which all life on earth depends.

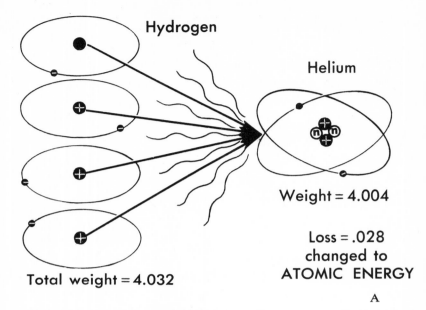

Figure 12-5.   Four atoms of hydrogen *fuse* to form one of helium (a). This is the basis of the *fusion*, or hydrogen bomb. The same process occurs in the sun (b). Thus we get from the sun the energy on which all life depends. *(Drawings by Mildred Waltrip from* The Physical World *by Brinckerhoff et al.,* © *1958 by Harcourt, Brace and Company, Inc.)*

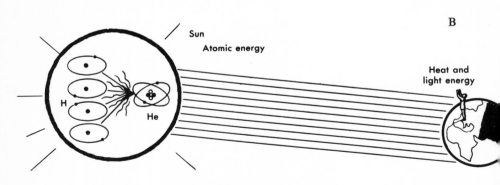

13

Studying the Stars

Look up into the sky on a cloudless night and try to count the stars in a small part of it. You will probably find it impossible, but at least you will be able to see the stars clearly enough to make a try at counting them.

Suppose, however, you could look at the portion of the sky with a telescope. You might see what is shown in Figure 13-1. This should convince you that studying the stars with the unaided eye is not very satisfying to the astronomer.

And to say that an astronomer uses a telescope is not really accurate; modern astronomers really need to be expert analysts of carefully made photographic records of the sky. Let's visit Palomar Mountain where the world's largest telescope is housed. Let's visit it on a moonless dark winter night when the cold air envelops the gleaming dome of the observatory (Figure 13-2).

THE TELESCOPE

Our astronomer, in his electrically heated suit, stops at the control desk and gives the engineer the position of the stars he plans to investigate that night. The engineer will

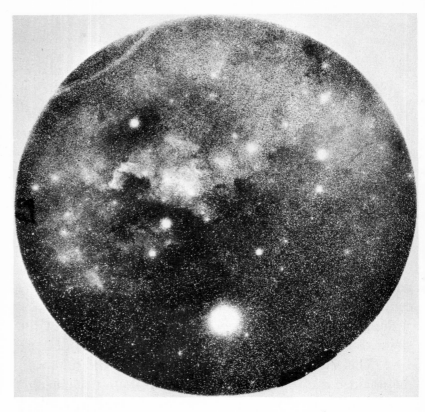

Figure 13-1.   Vast numbers of stars seem to dot the heavens. The naked eye itself is not keen enough to study individual stars.

(Yerkes Observatory)

handle the telescope, pointing it by means of mechanical controls to the position desired. Our astronomer steps on an elevator and presses the button that raises him to his observer's cage some seventy-five feet above the floor. He is barely comfortable in his cage (Figures 13-3 to 13-7).

At this point our astronomer is near the top of the two-hundred-inch Hale reflector, the world's largest optical telescope. Light rays are reflected upward and come to a point,

Figure 13-2. With the "Big Eye," the 200-inch Hale telescope, man has opened vast reaches for study.

(Mount Wilson and Palomar Observatories)

Figures 13-3 to 13-7.   As you read, study these pictures. Possibly they will give you a better idea of the astronomer's use of his most useful tool — the telescope.

Figure 13-3.   Inside the observatory — the huge Hale telescope in view.
(Mount Wilson and Palomar Observatories)

a focus that is, where the astronomer is seated in his cage.

If you've ever used a lens as a burning glass to burn a piece of paper, you know what bringing the sun's light rays to a focus means. Just where the sun's rays are brought together at a point — the focus — the paper will begin to smolder and burn.

Well, then, our astronomer is at the point where the light from the stars he is studying has been brought to a focus. And there he is, near the telescope's uppermost lens, its eye, armed with his photographic plates on which the heavens

Figure 13-4. The engineer and the astronomer discuss the position of the telescope for the work to come.

(Mount Wilson and Palomar Observatories)

Figure 13-5. Moving up and into position.

(Mount Wilson and Palomar Observatories)

Figure 13-6.   Stepping out of the elevator into the "cage."
(Mount Wilson and Palomar Observatories)

will be recorded. The beautiful, mighty telescope is used mainly to take pictures.

Now remember where our astronomer is. He is in a cage near the "eye" of the telescope; the eye is pointed at a chosen bit of the sky. Remember, too, that, meanwhile, the earth keeps turning. To stay pointed at the star — or bit of sky — he is studying, our astronomer must keep moving as well. So our telescope, weighing some five hundred tons, and the slit in the observatory dome and our astronomer in his observer's cage are kept moving by a delicate mechanism. The eye stays pointed at the moving star.

Each time the astronomer wants to make an observation, he sights at a bright star in or near the area he is studying. He carefully puts the photographic plate in place and opens

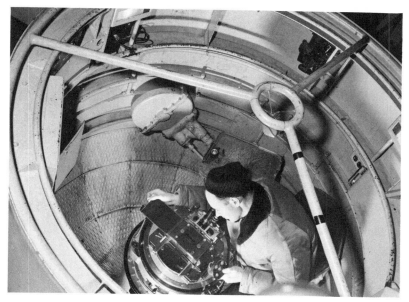

Figure 13-7.   Now the astronomer adjusts the camera's plate for the
right focus.   *(Mount Wilson and Palomar Observatories)*

the eye of the camera much as you open your camera for a
long exposure. After all, he isn't going to make a snapshot.
The light coming from the stars he wishes to study is very
faint and with so little light he will need a very long exposure — perhaps several hours, perhaps a whole night.

Therefore, he spends the night carefully checking each
new position, carefully setting his photographic plates, carefully adjusting the exact position in which the telescope
points. And all the time he moves as his telescope moves, to
keep the bit of sky in focus. Each observer of the group
using the telescope spends from two to eight nights a month
in this way.

What does the astronomer hope to find? Actually, analyzing the photographs in his laboratory — his week's work

with "The Big Eye" — will keep him busy for many weeks. What he will actually be analyzing is the light from the distant stars.

The Hale telescope is an amazing instrument. As you remember from your reading in Chapter 6, light travels at about 186,000 miles per second — nearly six trillion (6,000,000,000,000) miles a year. This is known as a light-year. The Hale telescope can probe into space for a distance of more than a *billion light-years*. If ever you have a bit of time, calculate how many miles this is.

One photograph can show only a very tiny section of the sky. One photograph, for instance, shows only about one-fourth the area of the moon. And the total area the astronomer could study in the Northern Hemisphere alone is at least 1,000,000 times that small area.

From his photographic plates our astronomer can learn a great deal. The starlight can be analyzed to determine the speed at which stars are moving across the sky by comparing two photographs taken at different times. Certainly the photographs can tell us more about our vast universe. Moreover, as astronomers fit the pieces of evidence together, they will begin to have an idea of the vastness of the universe. This idea is just beginning to form.

Now, of course, you personally cannot have access to the largest telescopes, but you can read about the different kinds.

One of the best sources of information is a planetarium — if you live in a city large enough to have one.

THE SPECTROSCOPE

Our astronomer who was photographing distant stars — or galaxies — had to work on a dark night, in the dark of the moon. And he worked with a few small patches of sky.

There are astronomers, specialists in analyzing the light from the stars. These astronomers (called spectroscopists) are experts in spectroscopy, the science that analyzes the spectrum (Figure 13-8). Let's look at this fascinating subject for a moment and see what it tells us about the universe.

Finding out what the earth is made up of is relatively simple. One can touch it, smell it, bring parts of it to the laboratory; there the chemist can analyze a chunk of it and discover the kinds of atoms in it. But how does one find out what the sun is made of — 93,000,000 miles away?

Clearly we have no way to scoop out a piece of sun. We

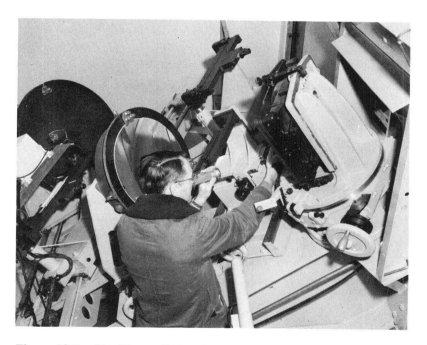

Figure 13-8.   Dr. Horace Babcock, of the Mount Wilson and Palomar Observatories, inspects the special equipment and plates for making spectroscopic analyses of stars.   *(Mount Wilson and Palomar Observatories)*

must analyze it at a distance. We can only do it by means of analyzing the light that comes from it — and from other stars as well.

Our spectroscopist checks his camera and his special photographic plate. He focuses carefully on one star and starts his exposure. This is a long and wearying time for, depending on the star being studied and what observations are to be made, the exposure may take from an hour to twelve hours — or even eight to ten nights.

The photographic plate is also a special plate. Not only is there an "image" of the light from the star on it, but also, as a check, the spectroscopist photographs on it, for comparison, the light from glowing iron in gaseous form. Thus he has on the plate the kind of light given off by the star and the spectrum of, say, iron.

The clue to what the spectroscopist sees lies in the *light* his plate captures. How can we analyze light? We are going to confess right here that we don't know what light really is.

You know light comes to us from the sun through more than 90 million miles of nearly empty space. Light behaves in two different ways at the same time — like waves and like snowflakes driven in a storm. It isn't that light sometimes behaves like waves and at other times like snowflakes. It is more mysterious even than this, for it can behave like waves and like snowflakes at the same time. Since no one has yet solved this puzzle, we will sometimes call light a series of waves, and at other times we will speak of it as tiny bullets of energy, which sometimes are called "quanta" or "photons." Also, we will not be embarrassed because we have made contradictory statements, for this is one of the many problems not solved. When we meet two things that are mutually contradictory and that are beyond our ability to harmonize, it is better to acknowledge it. We can say to ourselves we simply don't understand, but we hope that some day our researchers will help us to understand a little better. This is a much more satisfactory attitude than to imagine an answer that is hardly better than a dream.

By a somewhat complicated but very ingenious method in the laboratory, it has been discovered that apparently the only difference between the different colors, say, violet, green, or red, is in the number of microscopic waves of light that enter your eyes in a second. If these waves are extremely close together, your nerves are affected in a certain way and you call that sensation violet. These waves are so small that they cannot even be seen in a microscope. If you could see what is going on and if you laid down a foot rule in a beam of violet light, you would find that it took 62,000 of its waves to cover the space of one inch. That you will ever see one of these waves seems hopeless.

The number of waves per inch in each color in the rainbow has been counted in the laboratory. In order to give us the sensation we call blue, there must be about 55,000 waves to the inch; green, 48,000; yellow, 44,000; and red, 38,000. The very deepest red is about 33,000. When the waves become so long that less than about 33,000 of them make an inch, our eyes are unable to see them. They make no impression at all upon the nerves of our eyes, so that, for example, an alcohol flame that does send out such waves, and such waves only, is under certain conditions almost invisible.

There also is invisible light at the other end of this series of colors, for there are many waves that are so short and so crowded together that they are unable to give our eyes any sensation at all. They are like those piercing shrieks of some laboratory apparatus or some insects that are so shrill that they don't affect the drums of our ears. If waves are so short that it takes over 66,000 of them to make an inch, they are totally invisible to our eyes and are called ultraviolet waves.

From the sun we get beams of all the colors in a grand mixture, which we call white. The ultraviolet waves that come from the sun are, of course, invisible. Yet ultraviolet waves have a very remarkable effect upon us. If we are exposed to only a few of these rays, they are beneficial — they are the health-giving rays in concentrated form. These very powerful rays are nearly all absorbed by groups of oxygen atoms called "ozone," a layer of atmosphere beginning about thirty miles above the earth's surface. Also, most air contains minute quantities of ozone. However, only a small fraction of these waves get through to the earth. Too many ultraviolet waves would have a very bad effect upon us.

For several centuries men and women have known how to break up white light into colors by means of a prism, a three-sided piece of glass. It was in 1672 that Sir Isaac Newton established a firm foundation for the modern analysis of color. Raindrops and sunlight have made color from time immemorial; ancient man, who lived perhaps a million years ago, must have seen the rainbows as clearly as we see them.

If you let the light pass through a prism, that beam of light is spread out into a band of color, an artificial rainbow called a spectrum. If you let light go through several prisms and then through a magnifying glass, you can make a very long spectrum. The colors then are spread out in a long band so that sometimes each color is a foot or more in length. Just as in the rainbow, the colors are not sharply divided. Red merges very gradually into yellow, which almost imperceptibly becomes green. Violet occupies nearly half the spectrum. On the other hand, yellow and blue are scarcely more than narrow lines crowded between their big neighbors, red, green, and violet.

Such is the spectrum, the artificial rainbow, or a white-hot solid, as, for example, the filament of an electric bulb or a white-hot coal. When such light is passed through a prism, all the colors are always represented and in the positions in which we have just found them (Figure 13-9). But when we let the light of a very hot (incandescent) gas pass through a prism and then examine it through a magnifying glass, we find a very different situation.

As a rule, only a few colors are represented in the spectrum of a gas. A gas spectrum consists of bright lines of color. Each gas has its own peculiar group of colored lines. Some gases have only a few and some have thousands of lines of color. They are the "fingerprints" of a gas. And these "fingerprints" are what the spectroscopist studies.

When you see a certain group of colored lines in a spectrum, you know you are examining the light from a certain incandescent gas. These colored lines, grouped in such a fantastic manner, are like the combinations of a lock. When you know the meaning of each group, you can unlock the secrets of some distant flame that you might have great difficulty in analyzing in any other way. Each substance has its own group of color lines. Perhaps you wonder how each can be made to give light like a flame. If iron or nickel is placed in an electric arc, it will be turned to vapor or gas. The hot gas will give off light, and this light will always show peculiar groups of colored lines that are characteristic of that substance. So the spectroscopist can be sure that the lines he sees on his plate are always characteristic of the same substance.

For instance, sodium is a common metallic element. It is found in some of our most widely distributed substances such as salt, which is sodium combined with chlorine. When sodium gas is made incandescent by burning sodium in a flame, the spectrum consists for the most part of two bright yellow lines. These two yellow lines are characteristic of sodium gas. If you examine the light of any flame by means of a prism and find these two bright yellow lines, you may be very sure that the flame contains sodium. This is especially useful if the flame is beyond your reach.

The colors of the spectrum are bountiful in their gifts to us. Not only will they tell us what gases are burning in distant flames, but they also will give us the names of gases that surround the stars. Here on the earth the air is our atmosphere. The atmosphere of the sun is very large and exceedingly hot. Yet we know the names of sixty-two of its gases mainly through spectroscopy.

In the sun's atmosphere the spectroscopist has found gases of almost every kind — sixty-two have been identified. Some things that we usually think of as hard, like iron, are not only melted on the sun, but actually turned to gas by the tremendous heat. We find in the sun's atmosphere gases of iron, aluminum, tin, and lead. By this means we know the atmosphere of the sun contains gases of the following substances: hydrogen, helium, carbon, oxygen, sodium, magnesium, aluminum, silicon, potassium, calcium, manganese, iron, nickel, cobalt, copper, zinc, silver, tin, lead and many, many others. Clearly the make-up of the stars is very much like the make-up of our planets.

In the atmosphere surrounding the stars we find hydrogen, iron, helium, calcium, and many other gases. The spectrum would be a smooth band of color if it were not for the stars'

Figure 13-9. The upper band of color is the spectrum of an incandescent solid. All the visible colors are here arranged in the order of their wave length. It is the laboratory copy of the rainbow. The lower band of colors is the spectrum of a gas. Each gas has its own peculiar group of colored bands. (*From "Energy: Radiation and Atomic Structure" by H. B. Lemon, published in The Nature of the World and of Man; The University of Chicago Press. Courtesy of the University of Chicago Press*)

Figure 13-10. By means of the great telescope five feet in diameter at the Mt. Wilson Observatory the beam of white light from a star called Alpha Pegasi was spread out in a spectrum. Those dark lines mean that hydrogen gas is in the star's atmosphere. (*From a photograph of the prismatic spectrum of Alpha Pegasi—type Ao—taken at the Mt. Wilson Observatory with the 60-inch telescope. The spectrum was colored by Mrs. Alice Howard Park under the direction of Alfred H. Joy. Courtesy of the Mt. Wilson Observatory*)

atmosphere of gases. As in the sun, these gases absorb the color beams they themselves would emit if they were shining by their own light. Hence, the star spectra are covered with fine dark lines that spell by their peculiar code the names of the gases in their atmosphere (Figure 13-10).

What else can the spectroscope tell us about the stars?

We have noticed that the color beams, which are characteristic of each substance, appear as very fine sharp lines whose positions can be accurately measured. Also the dark lines, which take the place of those color beams under certain conditions, are very fine and sharply defined. Therefore, if a moving star approached us rapidly, we might expect to be able to notice a slight change in the position of these lines.

In 1848, a French astronomer, Fizeau, first described how these measurements might be made. Later, other astronomers selected a star that had in its atmosphere some well-known gas. For example, it is possible to take a star that has a spectrum crossed by the many dark hydrogen lines and compare its spectrum with that of a tube of hydrogen gas. You can so arrange the spectrum of the star and of the hydrogen gas that they both appear in the telescope side by side. In the star's spectrum there are the dark lines caused by the hydrogen in the star's atmosphere. If the star were standing still, continuous with these dark lines would be the colored lines of the incandescent hydrogen in the tube. However, if the star were moving rapidly toward us, the dark hydrogen lines would be moved a little toward the violet end of the spectrum, or, if the star were receding from us, the lines would be moved toward the red. This is called the Doppler effect, after the scientist who discovered it. All the while, the colored lines from the bright hydrogen tube would be the immovable standard to tell us whether the dark lines were shifted toward the violet or toward the red, that is, whether the star was approaching or receding from us. We now know that the stars are moving away from us at tremendous speeds; the dark hydrogen lines have shifted to the red.

Light travels 186,000 miles per second, as we have said before. If a star went half as fast, that is 93,000 miles per second, the light waves in front would be crowded together, one-half their normal distance apart. A deep red beam of color then would have twice as many waves per inch. Its normal 33,000 waves per inch would be increased to 66,000 waves per inch, but that is the frequency of the very last ray of violet we can see. Therefore, a star with such a velocity would have its dark lines moved clear across the spectrum. If the star, when it was standing still, was giving off nothing but red rays, that is, waves between 30,000 and 40,000 per inch, then, as it approached us at this tremendous speed, it would be of a violet color.

Of course this method of research tells us nothing about the movement of a star to the right or left. It merely tells us that the star is approaching or receding, and how fast.

The spectroscope can also tell us the temperature of the stars.

Wilhelm Wien, a German scientist, spread the light from a hot body into a colored spectrum, and then by a very delicate instrument, which we might call a kind of thermometer, he measured the temperature of each band of color. Also, he measured in this way those invisible colors, the infrared and ultraviolet. Curiously enough, these colors, visible and invisible, weren't all of the same temperature. There always was one point in the spectrum that was the hottest. The interesting thing was that the hotter the object giving off the light, the more this hot point in the spectrum moved toward the violet. Thus Wien discovered the principle that the position of the hot point in the spectrum can be made to give the temperature of the flame making the light.

This principle was immediately used to get the temperature of the furnaces in steel mills. Also flames that are inaccessible can have their temperatures determined in this way. A body does not have to be on fire to have its temperature measured by the spectrum; the application of this principle will give you the temperature of red-hot iron. Naturally, astronomers applied this method to some flames into which you cannot place a thermometer, such as those that surround the sun and stars. Thus, for the first time, we know the surface temperature of the stars, the planets, the moon, and the sun.

The Surface Temperatures of a Few Stars

Gamma of Cassiopeia	30,000° Fahrenheit
Vega	20,000° Fahrenheit
North Star	12,000° Fahrenheit
Capella	10,000° Fahrenheit
Beta of Andromeda	6,000° Fahrenheit

THE RADIO TELESCOPE

The most recent method of studying the stars, however, uses a different principle. If you kept your eyes turned toward the hot bright star you call the sun, you would be blinded. But if you turned one of your ears to the sun, people would think you wanted to get your ears tanned. Certainly the sun doesn't make "sounds." Well, it depends.

It depends on what you mean by sounds. And certainly the "sound" of the sun can be heard by appropriate instruments. The "sound" of the stars can be heard by a radio telescope — a new instrument in the armament of those who attack the secretiveness of nature.

Radio telescopes, big dishes as they are called, have to be quite large. Some are 50 feet across, others 80 to 250 feet. Many of them look like huge bowls (Figure 13-11). Usually they are built of sheet aluminum wedges fitted together very accurately. The bowl of the dish can swing on its base to face the parts of the sky being investigated.

Unlike the telescope, which gathers in light rays, a radio telescope gathers in radio waves — radio waves given off by the stars.

Figure 13-11.   The Jodrell radio telescope in England. Notice the large dish and central antenna. The Jodrell telescope first reported that Lunik II had reached the moon.   (*British Information Service*)

Light waves are very short waves; they are about 1/50,000 of an inch long. But you remember from your study of the spectrum that the spectrum is made up of a visible and invisible portion. The invisible (invisible to our eyes, that is) is both short waves and long waves. The short waves are those of ultraviolet and X-rays. The longer waves, the radio waves, vary from about one-fourth of an inch to several yards.

Because radio waves are so long, the dish of a radio telescope must be huge. Now if you examine the dish close up, you will see a pole, or a kind of antenna, at the center. Radio waves strike the dish, which acts like a mirror and is highly polished to reflect the waves to the antenna at the center (Figure 13-12).

In the antenna (some of them are called dipoles), the radio waves are changed into electric current and sent to a receiver much like a radio.

Of course, these waves produce a very weak current. But like the waves received by your radio, the current can be amplified so that the "noise" from, say, the sun, comes through with a hisssss and ssssputter. Or the electric current can be used to move an inked pen across graph paper and make a written record of the energy given off by the stars.

Studies of radio waves from the sun tell us, for instance, that the sun is larger than it was believed to be through evidence gathered from optical telescopes — that is, it thins out into an almost invisible layer, which still gives off radio waves — some very strong ones. Furthermore, it seems that the longer waves come from farther out in the corona.

A bothersome piece of evidence is that some radio waves come from sources that cannot be "photographed" through

Figure 13-12. Another type of radio telescope in the Naval Research Laboratory in Maryland. Here you can see the "dish" and "antenna" closer up.   *(© D. S. Kennedy & Co.)*

our powerful telescopes. What are these *presently invisible* sources of radio waves?

Are they stars too far away to be seen? New galaxies? Or clouds of gas? These clouds may be made up of hydrogen, perhaps; hydrogen seems to be the principal element of which the universe is made. This discovery of clouds of hydrogen seems very important. Since most such clouds do not give off light, they cannot be detected by optical telescope. But the hydrogen clouds do give off radio waves. And such clouds can be detected 50,000 light years away — on the other side of our Milky Way galaxy, a galaxy you are to learn about more fully in Chapter 15.

How will the map of the sky being made by radio astronomers tally with that resulting from investigations made through optical telescopes?

A whole new view of the universe is opening up. You are very lucky to be in on the beginning of these discoveries.

And now that you have an idea of the major tools in the astronomer's armament, let's swing out into the universe.

14

Out into the Universe — The Blue Sky

In the past chapters you have had an introduction to our solar system. You've been introduced to a bit of the vast universe astronomers have been discovering by means of eye, telescope, spectroscope, and radio telescope. And now it's time to go out into space.

The first thing you see as you look up — on a clear day — is the blue sky. To many of us this sky is interminable, but actually it's really only an envelope around the earth. What is the sky we see, really? Why is it blue?

When a beam of white sunlight enters a darkened room and happens to illuminate a painting, we see sometimes many colors — red, green, and violet. Yet when we touch the paint on the picture, we find it cold — no incandescent gas, no red-hot coals. That ray of white light has been changed into many brilliant colors by coming in contact with the paint. We know that certain paint, whenever it is illuminated by white light, always will give us those wave lengths we call red. Other paints will, with the same regularity, always send us waves of light that have the number per inch we call green, and so on, for a multitude of colors.

Here is a mysterious transformation that is taking place before us at every turn. We know something but not all about this secret. As we go on with this story, you will probably agree more and more with Edison, who said that we know only one-millionth of 1 per cent of all that can be known. Two hundred years earlier, Sir Isaac Newton compared all knowledge to a huge beach and claimed that he and his fellow men had merely picked up a few interesting pebbles here and there.

When rays of light strike a smooth substance, they are reflected just as a billiard ball bounces back when it hits the cushions at the edge of the table. If the substance is very smooth like a polished mirror, nearly all the light is reflected. If the incoming ray is white, then the reflected ray also is white, or if the incoming ray is red, the reflected ray is red. On the other hand, if the substance is full of microscopic holes as lampblack is, then almost no light is reflected. We say the incoming white light is absorbed. To a certain extent that is true, but soon the steady stream of energy from the light beam makes the lampblack warm. Then that black surface in its turn sends out waves, but these waves are so far apart that our eyes cannot notice them. We call them heat waves, for they affect our thermometers, and we can feel their warmth by the nerves in our hands. If we passed these rays through a prism, we would find they were beyond the deepest red called "infrared." Of course we couldn't see them. We know they are there in the spectrum because they affect a thermometer or some other delicate instrument for measuring heat.

The sun has sent down these millions of pellets of energy in serried ranks, as the gusts of wind in a snowstorm marshal countless snowflakes in company formation. Then they charge the rough surface of the lampblack. Their ranks are broken, but their fighting spirit, their energy, remains. The particles of the lampblack are made to vibrate, and this vibration causes a new set of energy waves to be emitted. However, the lampblack does not vibrate fast enough to send out energy waves so close together that they can affect our eyes. They are too far apart even to be called red, so we have named them heat waves. For this reason black clothes are warmer than white clothes, for the white is a better reflector and absorbs much less of the energy of the sun's rays.

Again, a beam of sunlight strikes a partially smooth surface. The sun drives his orderly battalions to the attack as before. The infantry, we will assume, enter the substance and are absorbed. Their energy is transformed into those long heat waves as before. This time, however, the cavalry refuse to enter. They dash off in another direction — they are reflected. Their ranks are so close together that they are known as color beams of violet light. So when they enter our eyes, they give us the sensation of violet. We call the paint that covered that surface violet paint, for we find that it always reflects only those waves of violet frequency and absorbs all others. Thus, an object is colored merely because it reflects certain beams of light to our eyes.

All surfaces are not quite so simple as these two examples. Some material reflects a variety of waves of different lengths. It gives us a blended color that our artists can analyze. They might say that it consisted mostly of reflected red and yellow rays with a very few of the violet. The others were all absorbed and their energy was turned into heat waves. When light becomes heat, we say it is "converted" into heat.

Our atmosphere is full of minute particles, extremely fine dust. Some of the short blue waves are reflected by these particles. The waves of other lengths pass them by and are little affected. Also the groups of atoms called "molecules" help to scatter the light. A molecule of water vapor consists of two atoms of hydrogen combined with one atom of oxygen. The reflected blue waves bounce from one particle to another until finally they reach our eyes from all over the sky. Hence, we say that the sky is blue, for wherever we look we get this blue sensation. When an aviator goes many thousands of feet into the air, he reports that the sky is darker than as seen from the surface of the earth. That means that he has gotten beyond the dust and most of the water vapor; the air above him is reflecting little light of any color, so it appears to him with much less than its usual brilliance. The sky then is blue only where there are particles to bounce back the short light waves that result in the sensation "blue" in our eyes.

When the sun is setting, it shines through many miles of dust-laden air. It has lost so many of its blue waves that the red now predominate, and the sun sets as if it were a red ball.

15

Out into the Universe — Stars in the Milky Way

On a clear night our sky is full of stars. There apparently are countless millions of them. If, however, you start to count those that are visible to the naked eye, you will be surprised how few there really are. Until the invention of the telescope, no one probably saw more than two thousand stars at any one time. But with this wonderful invention many more than 1,000 million stars can be photographed.

Even through the telescope, the stars are merely specks of light. They have no round disc like the sun when it disappears below the western horizon. They look through the telescope as they do to the naked eye, only very much brighter.

The planets are millions of miles from the sun and earth, but the stars are vastly farther away. We know these stars are round, but even with the most powerful telescope, we never can see their shape — they are always just brilliant points like distant electric lights.

As you might expect, the stars surround our solar system. On the spherical earth, only half the stars that are visible to the naked eye can be seen at *any one time*. However, at the equator it is possible to observe them all within a year. Our sun is one of these stars. All of the stars form a large cluster, in form flat as a pancake, or like a watch if you will. We call such a star cluster a galaxy. And the particular galaxy in which we find ourselves is called the Milky Way. At certain times it looks like a broad milky path that nearly divides the heavens into two equal parts.

For a couple of thousand stars we know the distances in miles because we have measured most of these distances as a surveyor would measure them.

We can measure very great distances in space by "light-years." A light-year is an imaginary measuring rod so long that it would take light traveling at about 186,000 miles per second one year to go from one end to the other.

It has been found that the nearest star, Alpha Centauri, is so far away that light from it, traveling 186,000 miles per second, takes about four light-years to reach us. It is thus said to be four light-years away or 24,000,000,000,000 (yes, 24 trillion) miles away. Only about a dozen stars are known to be within ten light-years of the earth. The Cloud of Magellan is 100,000 light-years away. Yet under the most favorable conditions light from Neptune can reach the earth in less than four hours, and light from the sun reaches the earth in eight minutes.

If the Egyptians had ever looked at the Milky Way through a telescope, they never would have thought that it was a river. In a telescope that white light disappears and we see nothing but myriads of individual stars.

This is another example of how deceptive appearances can be. It is very much like looking at a forest on the side of a distant mountain. From a long way off the forest appears to be a smooth dark-green band. Using a spyglass, you see the individual trees, which seem very close together. If you actually went to the forest, you might find the trees were so wide apart that you could ride a horse among them.

That the stars are all the same distance from us is also only a matter of appearance. Some are many thousands of times more distant than others. Occasionally three stars will appear to be close together and, perhaps, in a straight line. In reality, one star may be immensely farther off than the other two. They just happen to appear to us to be in a straight line and near together. As you might suppose, generally speaking, the fainter stars are farther away than the brighter ones. The bigger the telescope, the more of these faint, far-distant stars we can see. As a rule, the stars are as far from each other as we are from them.

It must have been far back in prehistoric times that men and women first noticed that there was a difference in the brightness of the stars. Probably tens of thousands of years passed before they gave names to the different degrees of brightness. The first list of stars that has been preserved and in which each star was given its name and brightness was made by Ptolemy about the beginning of the present era; that is, about 2,000 years ago. Ptolemy was a Greek who lived in Alexandria in Egypt. He belonged to a group of famous scientists and scholars. This early list consisted of approximately 1,000 stars.

The few brightest stars are classed as of first magnitude. The North Star is a typical second-magnitude star. The faintest star that you can conveniently see is about the sixth magnitude.

Generally speaking, the size of the stars is an indication of their brightness. If two stars of equal size and brightness are the same distance away from the earth, their brightness appears the same; if one of them is twice as far away from earth as the other, it appears one-fourth as bright.

Stars are classed generally in four groups depending on their brightness. In the first class are the Supergiants, then the Giants; then come stars of the Main Sequence, followed by the White Dwarfs.

Our sun is a Main Sequence star; most of the known stars are in this group. But the sizes of these stars vary from stars about ten times the diameter of the sun to stars, fairly cool ones indeed, about one-tenth in diameter. Most of the Giants and Supergiants do not have a surface temperature as hot as the sun. But because of their size, they throw out more heat. It is surprising to know that the stuff of which some of the Supergiants are made is so thin and so spread out that volume for volume it often weighs less than the air on earth.

Stars are generally found in groups, known as constellations. You will read more about these later, but for the moment you may want to know that Arcturus, the brightest star in the constellation the Herdsman (also known as Boötes), is a Giant star. The sun is a pigmy compared to it; Arcturus is some 96 times brighter and is about 21,000,000 miles in diameter, compared to the sun's 864,000 miles. The largest known star, a faint one in the constellation Auriga, is 2 billion 400 million (2,400,000,000) miles in diameter. Do you know what this means? Placed over our solar system, it would swallow up all the planets except the outermost three — Uranus, Neptune, and Pluto.

The Dwarfs are, of course, small stars; some of them are actually smaller than the earth. You remember from your reading in Chapter 12 that the Main Sequence star that is the center of our solar system derives its energy from the fusion of hydrogen atoms. Four hydrogen atoms fuse into one helium atom. Imagine that all the hydrogen has undergone fusion. What would happen? Four atoms become one. Obviously when fusion is over, the star must become smaller. And this is what scientists think has happened in the White Dwarfs. In fact, their atoms are now so close together that a pea-size bit of their stuff may weigh several hundred pounds. A bit of van Maanen's star, about the size of a baseball, would weigh more than 125 tons. White Dwarfs seem to have used up their atomic energy and have collapsed.

Some stars change their brightness and change their size amazingly. For instance, Betelgeuse (in the constellation Orion) may change suddenly in size from a diameter of 300 million miles to about 450 million miles. Its red color (it is called a red Supergiant) then becomes some 50 per cent brighter.

There seem to be three general explanations for the change in brightness. Long ago the Arabs watching the star Algol (in the constellation Perseus) saw it dimming regularly; patiently they studied it and saw that its dimming occurred every two days and twenty-one hours. When something occurs as regularly as this, it is best to look for an explanation.

Perhaps Algol dims and brightens because its hydrogen runs out and builds up every two days, twenty-one hours. No, the explanation is even more interesting. Algol has a dark companion star, or dim companion, that circles around it much as the moon circles around our earth (Figure 15-1). When the dim companion comes between us and Algol, it cuts off some of Algol's light. So Algol becomes dimmer. You might say Algol is eclipsed by its dim companion.

Astronomers have discovered that about one-third of the stars we see are really double stars. Endlessly they whirl

Figure 15-1.   The star Algol in the constellation Perseus has a dim companion. Both circle around each other. When the dim one eclipses the bright one, the bright one seems to grow dimmer. *(Drawing by Mildred Waltrip from* The Physical World *by Brinckerhoff et al.,* © *1958 by Harcourt, Brace and Company, Inc.)*

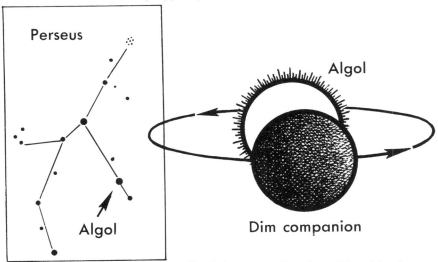

about each other. But not all of them are lined up like Algol and its mate, so we can't see the dimming from where we are.

Soon astronomers discovered other stars that changed brightness — but they were not double stars. The only satisfactory explanation was that these stars puff up, then shrink — but they do this in rhythm. Certain of these stars change in brightness with amazing regularity. In a few days they will go from bright to faint and back to bright again. Others will take a week or ten days. These stars are called Cepheid variables, because the first star of this class to be discovered was in the constellation of Cepheus. For instance, Delta, in the constellation Cepheus, takes about five and a half days to change from brightness to dimness.

What makes the light from some of these Cepheid stars variable is not thoroughly understood, but thanks to Henrietta Leavitt of the Harvard Observatory, and later to Harlow Shapley, we do know an interesting thing about them. The longer the star takes to change from one time of full brightness to the next, the more luminous is the star.

For example, if such a variable star takes 100 days to change from bright to faint to bright again, it is about 22,000 times as bright as the sun, that is, it is giving out 22,000 times more light than the sun. On the other hand, if a Cepheid variable has, say, only about five days between successive bursts of light, then it is only 700 times as bright as our sun.

To find the sun power of a Cepheid variable star, we have merely to count the days or hours between successive bursts of light. If the time between successive bursts of light is long, the star is really very bright; if the time is short, the star is not so bright.

Cepheid variables may be likened to flashing lighthouses, if you will. You know most lighthouses send out various long and short flashes, so that a sea captain can tell the name of the lighthouse by counting the number of long and short flashes. When he knows the name, he can look up the candle power of the lighthouse. In this way he can tell to some extent how far off the lighthouse is. If the captain counts two long flashes and one short one, he can find from his records that the lighthouse is on a certain rock and is 100,000 candle power. Perhaps to the captain it looks faint on the distant horizon. He might say: "That lighthouse is really very bright; it is, I know from my records, 6,000 times brighter than that lantern that is hung up on my mast. Yet the lighthouse and the lantern seem to me now to be about the same brightness. Since my lantern is 100 candle power, I can figure out how far away the lighthouse is."

So these Cepheid variables are sending their messages to the astronomer, just as the revolving lighthouses are sending their names and candle powers to the captain. Thus when astronomers know how luminous a star is and they measure how bright it looks, they can figure out how far away it must be. The astronomer can tell how much farther away the Cepheid variable is than the sun, just as the captain can tell how much farther away the lighthouse is than the lantern on the mast.

Thus the Cepheid variables are the flashing lighthouses of the universe. By them we can tell how far we can go out into space before we come to the dark outer space where stars are not seen by our telescopes.

There is still another explanation for a change in brightness of stars when neither the presence of a dim companion nor the Cepheid type of variable can be detected. What seems to happen is that a new star suddenly appears. This is called a nova or "new" star. Actually they are not new; they have just flared up (Figure 15-2). They seem to eject a cloud of very hot, very bright gas. Such a nova will fade out in a few days or weeks.

Most spectacular is the *supernova*. From its name you would rightly guess that this is a star that has suddenly become millions of times brighter — at times, a hundred million times brighter than our sun. It is possible that a supernova is a star blowing up — an awesome, furious, tremendous explosion.

Fortunately, there is not much chance that our sun will become a nova or supernova. If it did, our earth would become a cloud of vapor. This is hardly to be desired.

Apparently our cluster of stars is not fixed at all; they circle about each other; they change in brightness; they explode; all is action. Furthermore, the stars are not stationary at all. The stars are so far away from us that they hardly seem to move, but a spectroscope tells us differently. You remember from your study (Chapter 13) of the way the spectroscope analyzes the light from the stars that we can detect movement. So we learn that some of the stars move across the sky at 50 or 60 miles a second. Barnard's star has taken 180 years to move across the sky a distance about the apparent width of the moon (Figure 15-3).

Figure 15-2.   Do you see the expanding or flaring "bright clouds" around the nova? This one is the Nova Persei.

(Mount Wilson and Palomar Observatories)

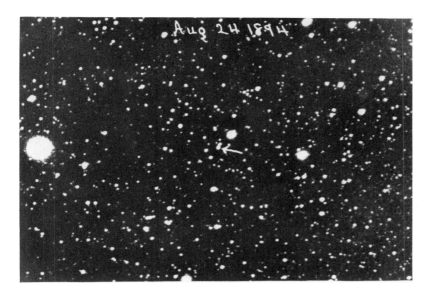

Figure 15-3.   The arrow points to Barnard's star. Notice the difference in its position on August 24, 1894, and May 30, 1916. Stars move — but to our eyes they move very slowly.   *(Yerkes Observatory)*

And the North Star, Polaris, is moving away from us at the rate of 15 miles every second. How much further is it away from you since you started reading this paragraph?

The stars, we have said, are grouped into constellations much as the United States is divided into states and Canada into provinces. Altogether there are 88 constellations. Knowing their formation will help you identify the stars. The first constellations to be named are in the Northern Hemisphere, because they were named by the Babylonians, Egyptians, and Greeks. In fact 48 constellations have come down to us as a result of the work of these people. Like the eastern states and provinces, the first to be settled, these old constellations have very irregular boundaries. In the Southern Hemisphere the boundaries of the constellations have only recently been determined. Like the western states and provinces, these newer constellations are bounded by straight lines and right angles.

Primitive men and women thought these groups of stars looked like animals or people. They must have had wonderful imaginations, for it is difficult for us to see much resemblance. In those days people had a number of favorite animals, and these animals were supposed to be governed by spirits. The bears were supposed to be controlled by a great bear spirit, the lions by a lion spirit, and the scorpions by a powerful scorpion spirit, and so forth. Each tribe, or sometimes each nation, had its favorite animal spirit. The spirits weren't always animals either; sometimes they were mythological men and women. It was natural that primitive man should want to stake out a claim among the stars for the headquarters of his favorite spirit. Some were more fortunate than others in their allotted territory. Scorpio, the scorpion, got a group of stars that looks very much like him.

Leo, the lion, got a fair location that resembles a great African lion, at least to a slight extent. Taurus, the bull, found himself in a group of stars that gave him a very good head and horns but left the rest of the bull's body to our imagination. Gemini, meaning "twins," in the acreage assigned to them by the Babylonians, were two bright stars side by side. The constellations Hercules, Virgo, and Orion bear very slight resemblance to the human form.

Of course you know that these constellations are purely imaginary as seen from the earth. You remember that when you see three stars in a row and close together, it doesn't mean that they are close together or really in a row. Two of them may be fairly close together and the third may be very far away. Sometimes on the side of a mountain you see a curious group of rocks that from a certain place looks like a human face. If you move up closer to this group, you will find that it is often merely a number of individual boulders and crags that are scattered over a considerable surface.

There are some interesting stars in the constellations that have no mythical association. Occasionally you will find a star that looks hazy or blurred. Through a telescope these blurred objects become marvelous clusters containing thousands upon thousands of sparkling stars. In the center of such a cluster the stars appear to be so close together that you cannot count them as individuals. One cluster, which is visible to the naked eye in the Northern Hemisphere, is called the Great Star Cluster of Hercules, for it is in the constellation of Hercules (Figure 15-5). In the Southern Hemisphere there is a still more brilliant cluster, also visible as a blurred star to the naked eye. It is called Omega Centauri, from the Greek letter w and the constellation of the Centaur. There are scores of these clusters, called "globu-

SUMMER SKY June 15, 10 PM

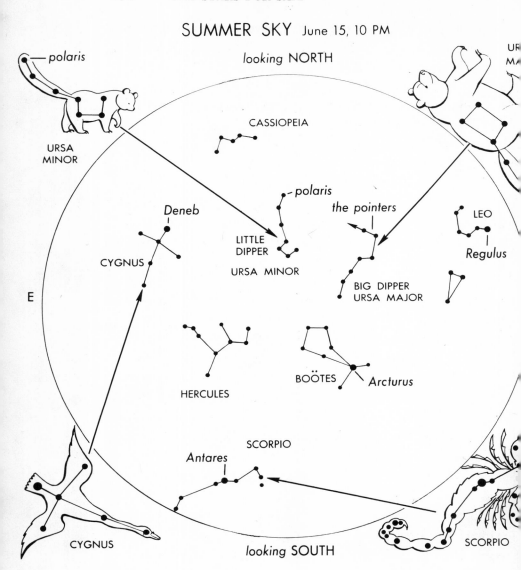

Figure 15-4. These star charts of the summer and winter sky are here to help you find some common stars. If you have a good imagination, you can group the stars into animal-like constellations — or other kinds of figures. The constellations Ursa Major (the Big Dipper), Ursa Minor (the

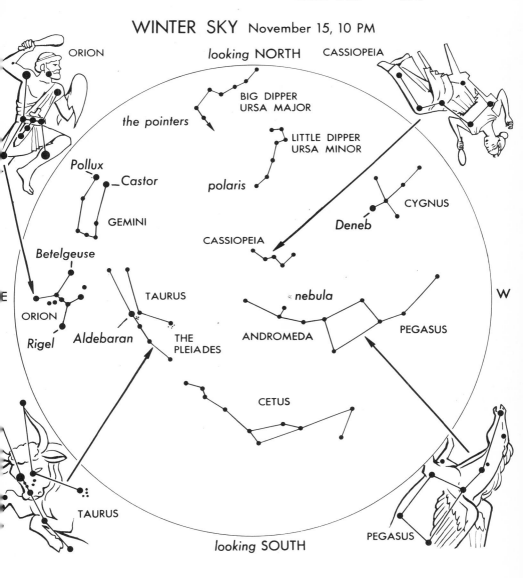

WINTER SKY November 15, 10 PM

Little Dipper), Orion (the Hunter), and others in the charts are such groups of stars. (See Figure 15-5.) (*Drawings by Mildred Waltrip from* You and Science *by Brandwein et al., copyright, 1950, 1952, 1955 by Harcourt, Brace and Company, Inc.*)

Figure 15-5.   When you locate the constellation Hercules in the sky, you may be able to find the huge star cluster in Hercules that is shown here. (Turn to the star chart in Figure 15-4 and note where the cluster will be.) *(Mount Wilson and Palomar Observatories)*

lar clusters," and they are symmetrically located with respect to the Milky Way, but to us they seem to concentrate on one side of the sky, because our solar system is off-center in the Milky Way.

Now examine the star charts (Figure 15-4) on pages 130 and 131. They represent for you the major constellations you will see in the Northern Hemisphere. As you observe the skies more and more, you will become expert at recognizing the stars in their constellations.

Astronomers have explored the extent of these stars. With their present instruments, astronomers find there is always a limit to the group of stars that surrounds us. A sufficiently large telescope will always look beyond that limit out into space, where for millions and millions of miles there are no stars.

Now by the help of the Cepheid variables, we can tell how far we must go in each direction before we reach this space that is so empty of stars. We find that the cluster of stars, our Milky Way, is shaped like a spiral disc, and our solar system is about halfway from the edge of the center of this large spiral (Figures 15-6 and 15-7). When we look out

Figure 15-6. A graph of the Milky Way. The Milky Way extends about 100,000 light-years. But notice that the great cluster of stars bulges in the center. Notice that the central bulge is about 20 light-years across. Our solar system is also about 20 light-years away from the farthest reach (left) of the Milky Way. Compare this with Figure 15-7. *(Drawing by Mildred Waltrip from* The Physical World *by Brinckerhoff et al., © 1958 by Harcourt, Brace and Company, Inc.)*

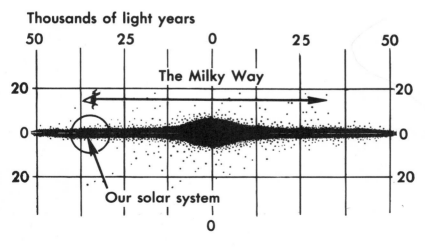

toward the edge of the disc in all directions, we see a vast number of stars. On the other hand, if we look through the thinnest part of the cluster, we see only a comparatively few stars, for example, in the direction of the Dipper in the constellation of Ursa Major, the Great Bear, or in the direction of the lion, Leo.

The sensation is something akin to walking through a long, narrow grove of trees. You walk halfway across this stretch of trees and then stop and look around. In either direction, before you and behind you, only a short distance

Figure 15-7. The Milky Way is shaped like a pancake with a bulge in the center. From the center it stretches about 50 light-years either way (100 light-years across). Notice where our solar system is to be found. (*Drawing by Mildred Waltrip from* You and Science *by Brandwein et al., copyright, 1950, 1952, 1955 by Harcourt, Brace and Company, Inc.*)

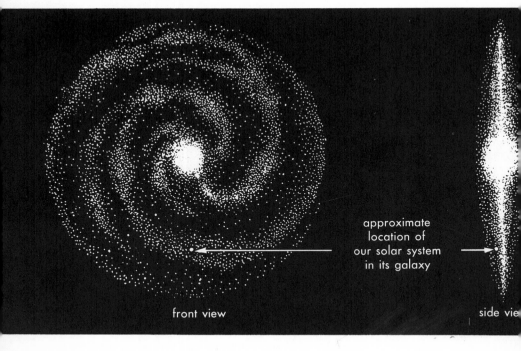

approximate
location of
our solar system
in its galaxy

front view   side vie

Figure 15-8. A nebula — quite bright. Why is it bright?
(Mount Wilson and Palomar Observatories)

separates you from the fields in which only a few trees are
growing. Of course you see these fields through the trees that
are surrounding you. Since the grove is long and narrow,
only a few trees obscure your view, if you look through the
narrowest part.

As you turn and look more and more lengthwise through the grove of trees, you see less and less of the wheat fields. You are looking through so many trees that your view of the wheat fields is becoming more and more obscured. If every tree held a lantern, you would say that as you looked through the longest part of the grove you saw a miniature Milky Way.

This watch-shaped star cluster, or galaxy, is enormous. Thanks to the Cepheid variables we know its diameter. It would take too much room on this page if we wrote its length in miles. So let us think about it in light-years. The diameter is about 100,000 light-years across. In thickness our galaxy is much less than that, perhaps 20,000 light-years.

This vast pancake of stars contains at least 1,000 million stars visible only through telescopes — besides those you can see. Now it is clear that a tremendous collection of stars as are found in the Milky Way galaxy would not stay flattened unless it was spinning — or rotating. Of course you cannot see this spinning because one trip of our star, the sun, all the way around — in a complete spin — takes about 200 million years.

Such a vast space seems inconceivable. The sun, we have said, an ordinary Main Sequence star, is about halfway from the edge to the center. The sun should not feel lonely; it is estimated by Harlow Shapley, the director of the Astronomical Observatory of Harvard College, that it has 100,000 million companions in the Milky Way, the galaxy in which you are a member.

If you look about in the Milky Way, you will see a luminous gas cloud now and then. It is luminous because it is near a hot and bright star; this luminous cloud of gas and dust you may know as a nebula (Figure 15-8).

Sometimes the clouds of gas and dust are not near enough to a hot star that can make them glow. Then this cloud cuts off the light of stars farther away and what you see is a dark patch such as the "Coal Sack" (Figure 15-9). We are going to call these dark clouds *dark nebulae,* and the bright ones, which can be seen, *bright nebulae.*

In the next chapter we will look at some of these cosmic clouds as we go beyond the Milky Way.

Figure 15-9.   A "Coal Sack" in the southern sky. Why is it dark?
(Harvard Observatory)

16

Out into the Universe — Beyond the Milky Way

The Romans called a cloud a "nebula," and we have used that word to describe faint patches of light we see through a telescope. We already have found by using a large telescope that some of these luminous "clouds" consist in part of stars. You know that on a clear dark night the Milky Way looks as if it were a band of fleecy and luminous clouds; yet in even a small telescope it becomes a mass of sparkling stars. The same thing is true of some nebulae. However, no matter how large the telescope, other nebulae do not become stars (Figures 16-1). Apparently they are real clouds — not clouds of water like our thunderclouds, but clouds of atomic particles, perhaps, sometimes shining by their own light, sometimes shining by light they have received from neighboring stars. They give the appearance of being illuminated by reflected light; but in reality they absorb and then emit, slightly modified, the light of nearby stars.

Some of these nebulae are nearby, astronomically speaking, and some, we have said, when examined with large enough telescopes, are seen to be galaxies. Those nearby are within the limits of our own Milky Way galaxy. These neigh-

Figure 16-1.   A cluster of far-distant nebulae as photographed through the Hale telescope. The distance is about 120 million light-years.
(Mount Wilson and Palomar Observatories)

boring nebulae certainly look like clouds. The two in Cygnus (the constellation of the Swan) look like cirrus clouds (Figure 16-2) — those long streams of white clouds that sometimes precede a storm. Then there is the famous Orion nebula surrounding the middle star in the sword of Orion (Figure 16-3). It is called Θ *(Theta)* Orionis. In English, that name would be Theta of Orion, who was a famous hunter. In the sky, Orion seems to be tantalizing the bull (Taurus) by holding up a lion's skin; while behind him the Unicorn is standing serenely indifferent to the turmoil around him.

Figure 16-2.   The nebulae in the constellation Cygnus, the Swan. Notice that they look like clouds.   *(Lick Observatory)*

At Orion's feet stands his famous hunting dog, Sirius. When Diana gave Orion those acres in the sky for his permanent residence, she little dreamed that underneath the surface there was a vast nebula. Orion, when he discovered it, must have felt like a North American Indian who has found oil under his reservation.

Some parts of the Orion cloud are bright, because it is excited to luminescence by hot stars within it. The Orion

Figure 16-3.   And this is the great nebula in Orion, the Hunter. (See the star chart on page 131.)   *(Mount Wilson and Palomar Observatories)*

nebula gives bright lines in its spectrum. However, somewhere in the sky between us and the Orion nebula there are dark clouds; at least they look dark to us. Such a one is the famous Dark Bay. If you could fly for years, so far that you would measure your flight in light-years, to the other side of the Dark Bay, you might find that it was after all a fleecy cloud — a bright nebula. From that other side it may receive a great deal of strong "sunlight" from neighboring stars. Thunderclouds on the earth behave in this way. When you can see the sunlight on a cloud, you know what a brilliant mass of fleecy whiteness it becomes. On the other hand, when the cloud of a thunderstorm comes between you and the sun in the afternoon, you can see only the dark side. Then the cloud seems to be a great black mass like the Dark Bay.

Apparently there are many of these clouds of gas that lie between us and some of the stars (Figure 16-4). We don't know much about them. They are almost incredibly large. It would take light, traveling 186,000 miles a second, many years to go from one end to the other of one of these dark nebulae. If the sun entered such a dark nebula, it might take tens of thousands of years to get out, for the sun is moving among the stars at only about twelve miles per second.

Perhaps a dark nebula consists of individual atomic particles driven hither and thither by sunlight and starlight. Like dust on a windy day, these stray particles may be gathered together in clouds. Sometimes these clouds absorb and then emit the starlight and help to make the sky brilliant, and sometimes they obscure the starlight and darken the sky. Among the stars these dark clouds of atomic particles may be the smoke nuisance of the galaxy.

Figure 16-4.   The stars of the Milky Way frame another great nebula —
the Great Nebula of the Ophiuchi. But note especially the clouds of gas
that show up as dark clouds or dark nebulae.

When we look at photographs of bright nebulae, they look
as dense as the smoke from a bonfire. Their appearance is
deceiving. In reality they are so light and rare that a whiff
of smoke would seem like lead in comparison. They are
sometimes called "cosmic clouds." Apparently we see the
sun and stars very clearly; yet there is evidence that we are
just emerging from a cosmic cloud. It may be a quarter of a

Figure 16-5.   And below is the famous Crab Nebula in the constellation
Taurus, the Bull.

(Mount Wilson and Palomar Observatories)

million years since the solar system entered this cloud, and
it may be several tens of thousands of years before we emerge.

One way of getting a picture of what is beyond our galaxy
is to imagine what we might see if we could go out into
space, go beyond our galaxy on our way to another. We
seem to see the pinpoint twinkling of stars in a black sky but
not one of these lights is a single star. Every one of them is a
galaxy, like our spiral galaxy; each one is made up of millions of stars. Not all are flattened spirals; some are blots or

smears of light; some are irregular in shape; some are flattened balls. They seem to cluster in some directions not in others where "space" stretches out in its blackness. The galaxies seem to like company.

Galaxies would seem close together but by the yardstick of space they are separated by about three to four million light-years of empty space. Perhaps this space is not "empty" in the sense of "nothingness," for after all we don't know too much about space. However, within a relatively short distance as the space of the universe is measured, that is within two million light-years of our Milky Way, thirteen other galaxies are to be found. One of these is the largest known galaxy — known as Andromeda (Figure 16-6).

Find the constellation Andromeda in the star chart (Figure 15-4). Now if you were to look at the clear sky at about 9 P.M. in January, or about 7 P.M. in February, you would see a fuzzy blob. You are looking beyond the Milky Way, past the stars that make up the constellation Andromeda, at the galaxy Andromeda. Cepheid variable stars in the blob assure us that it is a galaxy and that, further, it is about 1,500,000 light-years away. Remember, the farthest bodies in the Milky Way are not over 100,000 light-years away. Andromeda is then a cluster of stars very much like our own.

And like our galaxy it has its nebulae, its dust clouds and its variable stars. Does it have Main Sequence stars like our sun with their planets about them? Do these planets have living things on them. Perhaps living things like ourselves? Will we ever know?

Now perhaps you have a bit of an idea of the universe. You are one of two and a half billion people or so on one of nine planets around a medium-size star. Our sun is but one of about 1,000,000,000 (1 billion) stars grouped in a

Figure 16-6. This is the Great Nebula in Andromeda; it is worth searching for in the sky. Begin by finding the constellation Andromeda in the star chart on page 131. *(Mount Wilson and Palomar Observatories)*

spiral disc, our galaxy, the Milky Way. The Milky Way is but one of 100,000,000 galaxies — vast islands of stars — separated by vast spaces, so vast our minds cannot grasp it.

All these galaxies together make up the universe.

It was only a few centuries ago that our ancestors thought the earth and even the stars were only a few thousand years old. The world was very small and cozy and each star might reasonably be supposed to be acquainted with every other star. Then Galileo broke a hole in that medieval wall of prejudice and superstition by means of his telescope. Human beings began to realize the vast extent of the world. We have explored as far back in time as we have in distant space, and the end is not yet in sight.

We know now that the more distant galaxies are moving away from us, and from each other. The universe seems to be expanding. We know this because our analysis of the information taken from work with the spectroscope shows us that the color of the light coming from these galaxies is shifted toward the red. This is the familiar Doppler effect we learned about earlier. The farthest galaxies seem to be racing away from us at a speed hard to believe — 20,000 miles a second.

How do we account for this? One modern theory suggests that very early in the history of the universe it was squeezed together into a small volume — very, very, very hot. You might call it a sort of "cosmic egg."

This egg, full of atomic particles at a temperature of several billion degrees, exploded. The atomic particles could have combined very rapidly, in all manner of numbers, to give us all our present elements — and some elements perhaps that never lasted long enough for us to examine.

As the explosion continued, imagine a rapid cooling. Then the atom building stopped.

Galaxy-building could take place as the different parts of this expanding, whirling, eddying universe separated from each other into cosmic clouds. Each cloud might then form a galaxy. Within each galaxy, stars would form on the edges of the enormous mass of spiraling, swirling gas. And as the stars formed, so might planets form around the stars.

And so might our Milky Way galaxy have come into being, and our sun, and our earth.

17

We Step into Space

We began this book by suggesting that the first spaceman has already been born. And it is fitting to end this book by taking a first step into space.

The Russians were there first. On October 4, 1957, their little moon, about 22 inches across and weighing 184 pounds, their Sputnik, had been fired from the earth some 580 miles into space. A month later, the Russians launched another satellite, Sputnik II; this one, really the rocket's head, weighed about half a ton and carried a dog. This dog, the first living thing in space, lived for a week — but it reminded men that the space age had really been inaugurated. At last, man had an observation station above our earth's atmosphere. Certainly a rocket trip to the moon seemed a distinct possibility. Would you say a probability? Some people would! Some did not. But on September 13, 1959, the Russians hit the moon with Lunik II. Before that both the Russians and Americans had sent up rockets whose third stage went beyond the moon and into orbit around the sun. And there they are; two man-made objects, earth-made material, now joining the solar orbit. And now Lunik III circles the moon and the earth.

The Sputniks reached a speed of about five miles per second, hardly enough to go beyond the earth and around the sun or moon. Remember that to escape the earth a rocket — or any body — must reach a speed of seven miles per second. Already the Pioneer rockets sent up by the United States have reached that speed — but missed the moon. In the next years, rocket after rocket, satellite after satellite, will be shot up into space. Moon-shoot will follow moon-shoot. The next years will be exciting. But first many problems will have to be solved — and are being solved even as you read these pages.

Why is a rocket best suited for the job of moving beyond the earth's atmosphere — whether or not it carries a satellite or becomes a satellite? Unlike a jet plane, a rocket does not need oxygen to burn its fuel; it carries its own fuel and oxygen. It travels much like a cannon shell, but it starts slowly (we say, it accelerates slowly in the earth's atmosphere). Because of this slow start, it will not be heated to burning by friction within the earth's air envelope.

At present no single rocket has fuel enough to break away from the earth for the complete trip, so at present rockets are fitted together in two or three stages, piggy-back, to give the bursts of speed necessary (Figure 17-1). A good illustration of a three-stage rocket carrying a fourth stage, a satellite, is shown in the Thor-Able III rocket in Figure 17-1a and b. Notice that the rocket engines are in the first stage; they have a 150,000-pound thrust — that is, they push the rocket up with a force able to lift 150,000 pounds off the earth's surface. The satellite designed to be carried by the rocket is the satellite shown in Figure 17-1c and d. The paddles are designed to capture the sun's energy.

Now when the first rocket has used up its fuel, it falls

away or is cast off. At this point, the second rocket (the second stage) begins to burn its fuel, boosting the satellite even higher. Finally the second rocket falls away, and the third rocket (the third stage) carries the satellite — or whatever it carries in its cone — even higher. Now at last the final or third-stage rocket has succeeded in carrying the satellite with its instruments — radio transmitter or possibly a television camera — to its orbit. Now both the final rocket and the satellite or the satellite alone circle the earth (Figure 17-2).

The whole rocket head may become the satellite — as in the case of Sputnik II and III. Another whole rocket head was America's Atlas Rocket in Project *Score,* whose orbited portion weighed approximately 8,000 pounds (Figure 17-3).

But launching a satellite is not a simple job at all. First, we must have the fuel to send it far beyond the earth, beyond the air envelope of the earth. If the rocket were to stay in the air envelope, it would heat up very quickly and burn. This means also that we need special fuels. Even now the mixtures of liquid oxygen and hydrazine that are used are not as satisfactory as they might be. Experiments are being done with solid fuels, such as boron hydride. You will hear more about these new fuels as scientists develop them in the years ahead.

Once the fuel has been developed — and we already have satisfactory enough fuels to send a rocket head of 8,000 pounds into orbit — we need to be able to keep the satellite in orbit. Now you know from your earlier reading in Chapter 9 that the force of the earth's gravitational pull helps hold the moon in orbit. Otherwise, the moon would fly off toward the sun. This tendency of the moon to shoot off into

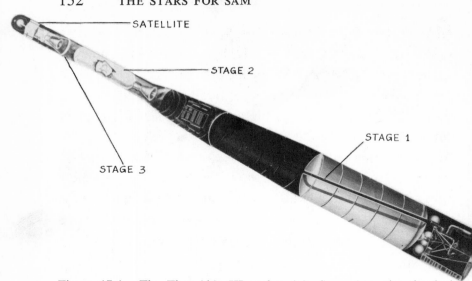

Figure 17-1.   The Thor-Able III rocket (a). Stage 1 carries the fuel
tanks. Stages 2 and 3 get the satellite into orbit. Stage 4 is the satellite
shown in (c) and (d). *(National Aeronautics and Space Administration)*

The Thor-Able rocket blasting off (b). Its satellite is in the nose cone.
(Official U. S. Air Force Photo)

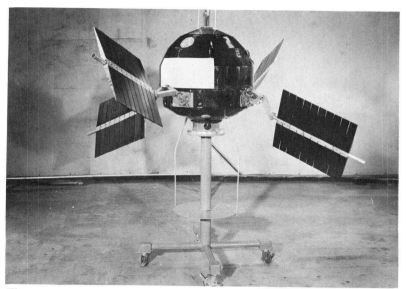

The paddle-wheel satellite (c). The paddles capture the sun's energy. Compare this way of capturing the sun's energy with the Russian satellite Lunik III (page 26). *(Official U. S. Air Force Photo)*

The satellite is packed with instruments (d). We are calling just a few to your attention, namely, the command box, the television circuit, and the batteries. The command box receives "commands" from earth. The other instruments detect different things found in space — for instance, rays and parts of atoms. *(National Aeronautics and Space Administration)*

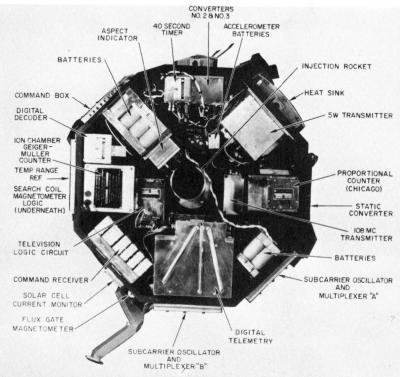

space is balanced by the pull on it of the earth. The moon is thus kept in orbit.

Now a satellite, even if fired out at five miles per second, would fall back to earth. If fired at more than seven miles per second, it would orbit around whatever body or bodies — the moon or, perhaps, the sun — happened to exert its pull on the satellite. But if the rocket is fired at an angle, the rocket will eventually turn till it is moving at right angles to the earth's pull. Then it must have a sideways speed around the earth of about five miles per second.

Now it can be calculated that a satellite 500 miles up moving at a speed of five miles per second will move five

Figure 17-2.   The path of a rocket. Do you see why a satellite sometimes has a third-stage rocket following it in its orbit? *(Drawing by Mildred Waltrip from* The Physical World *by Brinckerhoff et al.,* © *1958 by Harcourt, Brace and Company, Inc.)*

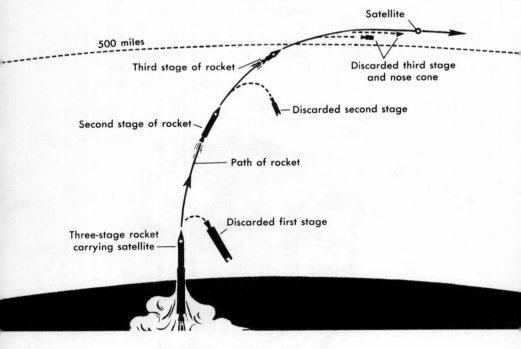

Figure 17-3.   The mighty Atlas used to put into orbit the satellite in project *Score*. Assume the men below to be about six feet in height and you get an idea of the size of the rocket. *(Official U. S. Air Force Photo)*

miles ahead in a straight line but will fall toward the earth at about 12 feet per second. So a satellite will tend to move around the earth and fall slowly toward it. Eventually, it will re-enter the earth's atmosphere and burn up — that is, if it continues to be made up of present materials. Newer materials are being developed that may not burn up; then a satellite will return to earth slowly enough not to endanger living things that may be in it. And soon living things, perhaps men, will go up in rockets — and manned satellites. They will want to, and need to, return safely to earth.

As a satellite goes into orbit, can it be seen? Yes, if it is large enough. And even if it isn't, it can be tracked. Observations of a satellite can be made in three ways — by looking, by photography, and, of course, by radio.

Suppose now you join *Operation Moonwatch* and help search for satellites. America's Atlas (Score) could be seen as a moving "star" even with the naked eye, certainly with a pair of binoculars. But the small experimental satellites had to be tracked. Many observers, young and old, were organized to help track satellites to get data for Project Vanguard, the satellite project of the U.S. This operation has been called *Operation Moonwatch* (Figure 17-4).

If you were an observer in Operation Moonwatch, you would be part of a team; each member is expected to report *the time* he or she saw the satellite, *the direction* in which the satellite was moving, and *the place* from which he observed it. Figures 17-4 and 17-5 show you such observers at work. Apparently, the most useful observations give the observer's position and the time the satellite moved across his meridian, that is, the north-south line overhead.

Now when many of these observations, made through binoculars, are reported, the direction of the satellite can be

Figure 17-4.   This is a Moonwatch team in Columbus, Ohio. Each viewer is trained to report when he sees the satellite. All the viewers' reports are then put together and the course of the satellite or "moon" is plotted.
(Smithsonian Astrophysical Observatory)

plotted. This isn't too easy. After all, the experimental satellites we've been shooting up are about the size of a basketball. A few hundred miles away the light reflected from one of these is very faint — as bright as the faintest star. But once the direction is known and ascertained, special cameras are trained on the satellites (Figure 17-5).

Once these cameras are trained on a satellite, a special timing mechanism (turned by a motor) can be set to follow the satellite. A picture of Sputnik I was tracked by such a camera (Figure 17-6).

If a satellite sends out signals by radio, observers can tell when it is over their heads. But receiving radio signals de-

Figure 17-5.   Satellite-tracking cameras like this one are being used to plot the orbits of satellites with great accuracy.

(Perkin-Elmer Corporation)

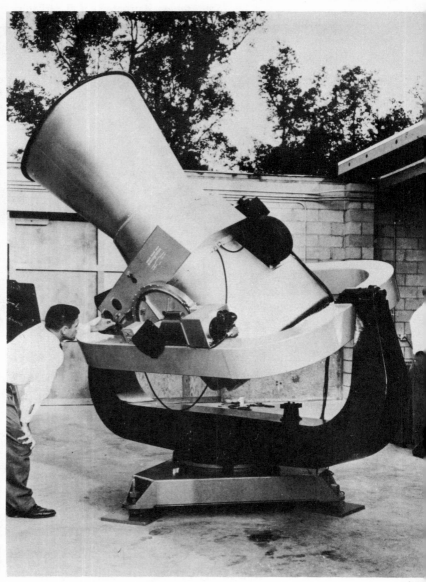

pends on the transmitter in the satellite, and this depends again on the battery. On the other hand, a chemical battery can be recharged by the sun's energy, and this is how a modern satellite's battery is indeed recharged.

Radio signals help tell observers only where to look. But signals from a satellite can be received over a very large area. For instance, when the satellite is about 500 miles above the earth, its "beeps" can be heard anywhere over the United States. By using radio signals and observers and cameras, a satellite can be tracked.

In order to watch a satellite, you will have to reserve some time during twilight, for you won't be able to see it at night

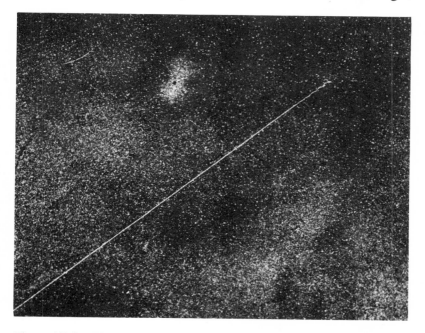

Figure 17-6.   The streak you see is Sputnik, the Russian satellite, passing near Canberra, Australia. The streak, which extends from lower left to upper right, was made by a continued camera exposure. Notice the star-studded background.   *(Wide World Photos)*

Figure 17-7.   Study this diagram carefully. Do you see why you need to search for satellites during twilight? *(Drawing by Mildred Waltrip from The Physical World by Brinckerhoff et al., © 1958 by Harcourt, Brace and Company, Inc.)*

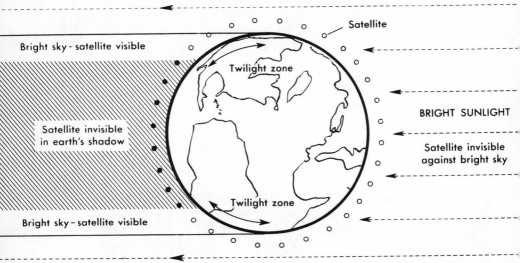

or during the day. At night, both you and the satellite are in a shadow, the earth's shadow, and light cannot therefore be reflected from it to you. During the day, the sky is too bright. During twilight, the satellite alone is still in sunlight; our sky is dark and we are in shadow. Then it can be seen — and tracked (Figure 17-7).

What is the value of satellites anyway? First, a satellite, or a rocket in orbit, properly designed, is a research laboratory. It is packed, literally packed, with instruments that send back information about space. This information is fed into giant mechanical brains, which sift it and feed it back to scientists who interpret it.

As you have learned, your life is affected by bodies in space. The moon affects tides; plants cannot make food without sunlight; cosmic rays are bombarding you even

Figure 17-8.   A design for a space station. The rotating space station (as yet only half completed) is being assembled. At the lower right is a completed space station out farther in space. At the lower left is a rocket that is bringing the parts for building the space station. At the upper left another rocket bringing more materials and spacemen has left the earth. Can you see the spacemen? Some of them are on the rocket; some are on the space station; at least one of them is out in space hauling a part of the space station.   *(American Bosch Arma Corporation)*

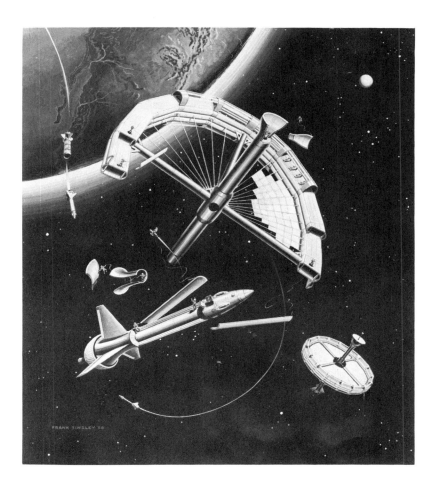

now. And what of meteors? Now satellites can send back information relating to these questions as well as information on:

The radiation belt around the earth. You must have read that Explorers I and II sent back information of the existence of a deadly belt of high radiation surrounding the earth. This would make it difficult to send men into space unless the rocket were shielded with a very thick layer of lead. This, in turn, would make it impossible to send a rocket out into space because too much fuel would be needed.

Recently, however, evidence has been obtained from satellites that there are "holes" in this belt, mainly along the North and South Poles.

We could not have evidence of this radiation belt without the information sent back from satellites.

The true "map" of the earth. Is the earth really round? We know that the earth has a bulge of some thirteen miles around the equator. But is the bulge evenly distributed? Did the moon really come off from the earth? If so, would there be a place, say, an indentation, where it originated?

The height of the atmosphere. How high is the atmosphere? We know that although half of all our air is pressed into the first 3½ miles from the earth, there must be some air at about 60 miles because meteors burn up around that height. Auroras go as high as 300 miles. But what is the composition of the air up there? Is there more hydrogen at the outer rim of the atmosphere?

The weather. Can the satellite predict weather far enough ahead to be helpful to man? Weathermen think that part of the answer lies in knowing more about how sunlight changes the top of the atmosphere. Who knows but that one day we will be able to predict the weather months ahead!

The sun. You read about the sun's corona in Chapter 1. How far does it really extend? How far do ultraviolet waves — and other rays and particles — come out of the corona? Do they affect the upper parts of the atmosphere?

Meteorites. Even now, as satellites go up on their exploratory forays, their special equipment records the ping-ping of meteorites hitting their sides. These are very tiny, but we also know that there are larger ones that hit the earth's atmosphere each day. At their speed of some twenty to forty miles a second, these meteorites could wreck a spaceship — or a rocket to the moon. Satellites may give us information on the nature and size of meteors.

The other side of the moon. We see about 59 per cent of the moon's surface. What does the other side of the moon look like? One of our Pioneer rockets just missed entering the moon's gravitational field; another, for all we know, is somewhere out in space. It missed the moon altogether. The Russian Lunik I also missed the moon; Lunik II hit somewhere near the Sea of Tranquility (Figure 2-2); Lunik III went into orbit around the moon and sent back pictures of the other side (Figure 2-4).

Evidence gathered by satellites may give us some information concerning these questions. And while satellites are gathering this information, we may also get evidence about the origin of cosmic rays, some of which come from the sun.

The conquest of space. Sooner or later, man will go up into space. Werner von Braun, one of the foremost experimenters of our space age, working out of the Army Ballistic Missile Agency, Redstone Arsenal, at Huntsville, Alabama, predicts that we could put up a space station within the next few years — if we wished it. Now a space station is a satellite, although it is different from the ordinary small satellite or rocket. It is like a huge hollow doughnut with spokes as shown in Figure 17-8. The parts to make such a satellite could be shot up into orbit about 1,000 miles above the earth by rocket. There the different parts of the satellite would be assembled into the space station you see in the figure. Who would assemble it? Men, of course.

These men would be shot up in manned rockets into the orbit where the parts are already revolving. Men in space suits like those shown in Figure 17-9 could step out into space and push themselves about with air jets, which work on the principle that every action will result in a reaction. Thus even the slightest jet of air shot out by the air gun will cause the spaceman to move in the opposite direction. Once the space station is assembled, men could live in it in comfort. This space station could then be a good place to serve as a take-off, a spaceport, for more distant places in space.

The space station may be about 300 feet across and the rim (or doughnut) may be 30 feet in diameter. Its parts, as we have said, can be readily assembled by spacemen, who — like the parts they assemble — will be weightless. As soon as the frame is assembled, more and more parts will be shot into space till finally a large doughnut-shaped apartment house will be revolving about the earth every two minutes or so. It will spin (rotate) at about three miles a minute, which will simulate a field of gravity. Otherwise, the spacemen will not be able to walk upright, coffee will not stay in cups, tables will float, and so will the inhabitants. Our spacemen and spacewomen will have to be very able, specially trained people.

As we have said, seven Americans (astronauts) have already been chosen. One morning, one of these seven shown in Figure 17-10 will get into his capsule; he will be fully pre-

Figure 17-9.   A space suit for future spacemen being tested. Perhaps this is what the first well-dressed spaceman will wear.
(Official U. S. Navy Photograph)

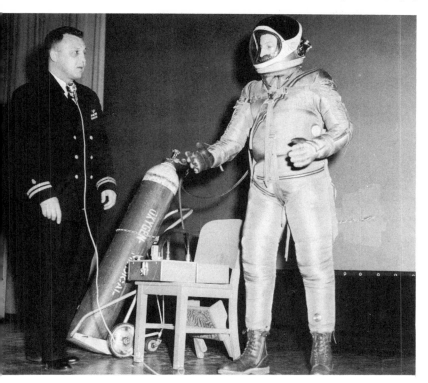

pared. He will be catapulted into space 100 miles or so and then he will plunge into the Atlantic Ocean. The nose cone of the rocket similar to the one in which the astronaut will be strapped has already been safely recovered. A pressure suit will protect him from the terrific change in pressure. Instruments designed to bring him safely home will pack the space around him. The astronauts will have undergone all sorts of tests (Figure 17-11). They will be ready. Look at them — physically fit, well-educated, and ready.

Figure 17-10.   The seven U. S. astronauts, one of whom will be the first to go out into space from our country. Meanwhile, they are preparing themselves through hard work — mental as well as physical. Possibly one of them will go up in the capsule Leroy Gordon Cooper is holding. From left to right, seated: Virgil Grissom, Malcolm Scott Carpenter, Donald Slayton, and Leroy Gordon Cooper, Jr. Standing: Alan Shepard, Jr., Walter Schirra, Jr., and John Glenn, Jr.

(National Aeronautics and Space Administration)

Can men take all this? Sputnik II showed that a dog could take it for about a week — then it died. Scientists in Russia and the United States have sent mice up in rockets and obtained valuable information. And on December 13, 1958, the United States Army sent a squirrel monkey 2,500 miles into space but failed to recover the nose cone that had in it the cabin holding the monkey. Nevertheless, valuable measurements were taken of the monkey's blood pressure and heart action, pulse and breathing rate. Soon after that, two monkeys, Able and Baker, were sent out into space — and safely recovered (Figure 17-12).

And now man has hit the moon and sent a rocket into orbit around it. We should acknowledge these remarkable feats performed by the Russians, but the Russians were using knowledge perfected in all countries. It was an American, Robert Goddard, of Clark University at Worcester, Massachusetts, who developed the first liquid-field rocket in 1931. But Goddard would have been the first to acknowledge his indebtedness to Konstantin Tsiolkovsky, a Russian who published one of the first serious works on space travel (astronautics) early in this century. And Tsiolkovsky in his turn would have acknowledged his dependence on Sir Isaac Newton, who stated the laws of gravity. And Sir Isaac in his turn would have stated his own dependence on the work of Johann Kepler, who in 1609 developed the laws that men use in calculating the motion of heavenly bodies. The work of science is the work of many men in many different countries.

Nevertheless, the Russian feats were notable. All present evidence points to the fact that the Russians did hit the moon — although in reality it will be difficult to be absolutely certain since the rocket ceased sending signals once it hit the moon. You may remember that Jules Verne, in 1865, told of an imaginary trip to the moon by rocket in a book called *A Trip to the Moon*. His "missile" was fired from a 900-foot tube sunk into Florida rock. Strangely enough, Verne's imaginary moon expedition was jointly sponsored by the United States and the then Imperial Russian Government.

The feat, then, is accomplished. A sphere of unknown size, weighing 858 pounds, crashed into the moon near the Sea of Tranquility (Figure 2-2). It hit at about the speed of

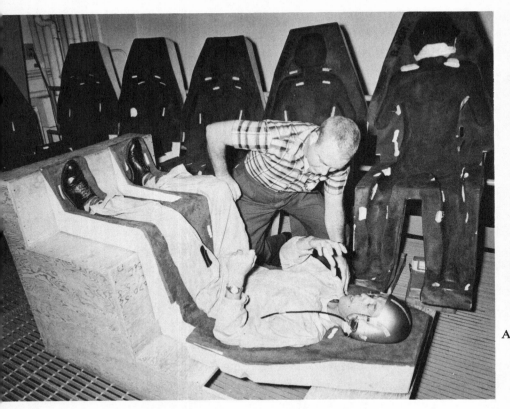

A

Figure 17-11. Astronaut Alan Bartlett Shepard, Jr., tests the molded foam support in which he will be strapped in his capsule when and if he hurtles out into space (a).   *(Official U. S. Navy Photograph)*
In (b), a photo of a model of a space capsule, you see the way he might appear on his way out into space.   *(McDonnell Aircraft Corporation)*

7,500 miles at 2 minutes and 24 seconds after midnight on September 14, 1959, Moscow time. This was 2 minutes and 24 seconds past five New York time — or three hours earlier Los Angeles time.

Mark well the time. The moon had been reached with a man-made missile; 236,875 miles had been traveled in about 35 hours (Figure 17-13). And soon man himself must fol-

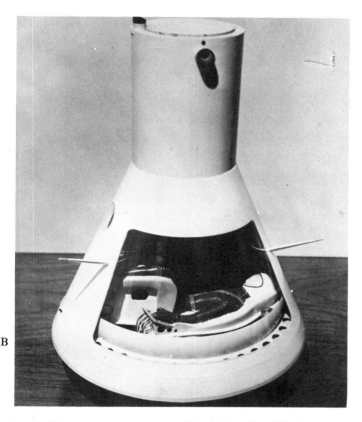

B

low. Furthermore, a satellite, Lunik III, has now photographed the back of the moon (Figure 2-4). Lunik III was launched by the Russians on October 4, 1959, at 7 P.M. Russian time (12 midnight New York time). The 51-inch satellite is shown in Figure 2-5 (page 26). It takes part of its energy from the sun through solar batteries; it is packed with instruments, particularly cameras, which can be triggered from earth.

Experiments have been done on earth, on the ground, and in special chambers that duplicate conditions in space. But till men have been shot up into space and have returned to tell the tale, we shall not know whether men can take it. Russian and American scientists both are now carrying on experiments; either national group of scientists may soon be successful.

You and we are all very fortunate to be living in one of the great ages of discovery. Man is to challenge space.

Why? Perhaps because man is the seeking animal — always seeking for knowledge or adventure. Perhaps because space is there and man must ever conquer new heights. You remember the mountain climber who was asked why he wanted to go to the top of Mt. Everest; his answer was classic. "Because it is there."

Figure 17-12.   Monkey Baker, an American-born squirrel monkey, traveled with monkey Able in the nose cone of a Jupiter rocket. This picture shows one of several monkeys (wearing his space helmet) in training for the flight.   (*Official U. S. Army Photo*)

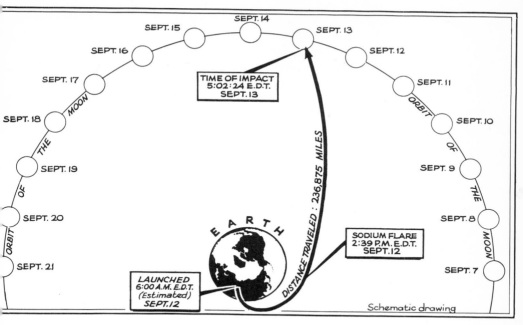

Figure 17-13.   The path of the Russian missile that hit the moon. Notice
how carefully calculations had to be made in order that the nose cone of
the missile might hit the moon 236,875 miles away.

(© New York Times, September 14, 1959)

Or because of still another reason. Project Score, our satellite, weighing some four tons, had as its major objective
the improvement of communications. Its tape recorder received messages from the earth and rebroadcast them to
other stations on earth. And what was the first message sent
from space to earth, on December 19, 1958, some 600 miles
above earth? It was the voice of the President of the United
States wishing all who heard, "Peace on earth, good will to
all men."

Perhaps the major reason for some men's desire to get
out into space is to assure peace on earth.

Index

and theories of origin of planets,
14-16, 18
Sunspots, 8, 9; *illus.*, 7
Supergiant stars, 121
Supernova, 125
Swan constellation, 139

Taurus constellation, 129
Telescope, 93-100; *illus.*, 95, 96, 97,
98, 99
Thermometer, 115
Thor-Able III rocket, 150; *illus.*,
152
Thrust, of rocket, 150
Titan, 14
Tracking of satellites, 156-160;
illus., 157, 158, 159, 160
Trip to the Moon, A, 167
Tsiolkovsky, Konstantin, 167

Ultraviolet waves, 104, 111, 163
Universe, in "cosmic egg" stage,
147

Uranium, atom of, 89
Uranus, 10, 18, 39, 54, 58, 60;
illus., 11, 55
Ursa Major, 134; *illus.*, 130-131
Ursa Minor, *illus.*, 130-131

van Maanen's star, 122
Vanguard Project, 156
Vega, surface temperature of, 109
Venus, 10, 16, 32, 36-39, 41, 60;
illus., 11, 37
Verne, Jules, 167
Virgo constellation, 129
von Braun, Werner, 163

Water, molecule of, 86, 117
Weather prediction, by satellites,
162
Whipple, Fred, 18
White Dwarf stars, 121, 122
Wien, Wilhelm, 108, 109

X-rays, 111